S0-ADN-658

# lesbian words

**rk** A RICHARD KASAK BOOK

# lesbian words
## state of the art

*Edited by Randy Turoff*

*Lesbian Words: State of the Art*
Copyright © 1995 Randy Turoff

"How Menstruation Fashioned the Human Body," from *Blood, Bread, and Roses* by Judith Grahn. Copyright © 1993 by Judith Rae Grahn. Reprinted by permission of Beacon Press.

"The Vampire Lovers" from *Vampires and Violets: Lesbians in Film* by Andrea Weiss. Copyright © 1993 by Andrea Weiss. Used by permission of Viking Penguin, a division of Penguin Books USA Inc.

"Butch Icons of the Silver Screen" by Jenni Olson from *Dagger: On Butch Women*, (Cleis Press, 1994). Edited by Lily Burana, Roxxie, Linnea Due.

"Chic by Nature" Copyright © 1995 Randy Turoff

"F2M: The Making of Female Masculinity" by Judith Halberstam from *Lesbian Postmodern* edited by Laura Doan. Copyright © 1994 Columbia University Press. Reprinted with permission of the publisher.

"Campaign Diaries" by Eileen Myles first appeared in part in *Paper Magazine*. "Letter to Madonna" previously appeared in the journal *The New Censorship* in 1992.

"Believing in Literature," by Dorothy Allison from *Skin: Talking About Sex, Class & Literature* (Firebrand Books, Ithaca, NY) Copyright © 1994 by Dorothy Allison.

"Because Silence is Costly" from *Forty-Three Septembers* by Jewelle Gomez (Firebrand Books, Ithaca, NY). Copyright © 1993 by Jewelle Gomez.

"First Ed" from *The Apparitional Lesbian* by Terry Castle. Copyright © 1995 by Columbia University Press. Reprinted with permission of the publisher.

"South Side" Copyright © 1995 Camille Roy

"Slipping" is from *Melting Point*, by Pat Califia, Copyright © 1993 by Pat Califia. Reprinted by permission of Alyson Publications, Inc.

All Rights Reserved

No part of this book may be reproduced, stored in a retrieval system, or transmitted in any form, by any means, including mechanical, electronic, photocopying, recording or otherwise, without prior written permission of the publishers.

First Richard Kasak Book Edition 1995
First Printing October 1995
ISBN 1-56333-340-6

Cover Design by Dayna Navaro

Photo Credits/Top to Bottom, Left to Right:
Judy Grahn (Chris Felver), Eileen Myles (Dan Larkin), Robin Podolsky (Chuck Stallard); Dorothy Allison (Jill Posner), Judith Halberstam, Canyon Sam (Bob Hsiang), Terry Castle (Jocelyn Marsh); Camille Roy (Angela Romagnoli), Andrea Weiss (Ekko von Schwichow), Jenni Olsen (Ingin Kim); Jewelle Gomez (Val Wilmer), Randy Turoff (Erin O'Neill), Pat Califia (Phyllis Christopher).

Manufactured in the United States of America
Published by Masquerade Books, Inc.
801 Second Avenue
New York, N.Y. 10017

## Acknowledgments

To Rondo Mieczkowski and Sherry Dranch, for continual
loving friendship and professional support. To my family
for their tried and true faithfulness. And thanks to my
good buddies, especially Coral and Lee, for being there
through this project.

# Contents

## Part Two: Personal Reflections

# lesbian words

# Introduction

*Randy Turoff*

This anthology is intended to be an up-to-date collection of some of the best lesbian writing coming out in print. Some of the essays or versions of them have appeared in recently published books, in anthologies, and as excerpts in magazines. Much of the work is being presented here for the first time. By and large, these are literary essays, conscious of style and of the quest for emotional integrity.

As a journalist and cultural reporter for the last decade, and as an "out" lesbian living and working in the community for a number of years, I've followed the evolution of trends in politics and the arts, as codified by the literature, films, videos, and theater being produced by queer artists. It is my pleasure, as an editor, to be able to present this collection for your thoughts and enjoyment, whether you're a student of lesbian/gay/transgender or women's studies, a writer, a reader, a colleague, or a nongay person interested in exploring images and issues of the day through lesbian perspectives.

Although each contributor is lesbian oriented, and the overall flow of the anthology posits an organic body of work, there are remarkable differences and disjunctions between the individual authors. The styles, voices, and the concerns of the lesbians behind these essays are as varied as the practice of lesbian sexuality. Also note that this collection is limited by necessity and by design, and that it represents a greater proliferation of fine work being produced and published, as we speak, as we read. Lesbian words are finally asserting an undeniable presence in the literary canon.

The work presented here is eclectic and ongoing. It is held together like a hologram, projected from this moment of evolution in lesbian consciousness. The intended overview is derived from differing points of view; reflections bouncing off of each other to create the overall in-depth picture of how we look, how we're seen and how we are.

The book is therefore not traditionally framed-in by subject matter, theme or a prescribed agenda. The themes emerge from within the individual pieces and echo intertextually from essay to essay.

As the editor, I've selected work from among the writers I like to read—lesbian authors who play with ideas and who write the kind of creative nonfiction that inspires me as a reader, a critic, and as a "fellow" writer.

Part One opens with Judy Grahn's "How Menstruation Fashioned the Human Body" from her brilliantly iconoclastic book, *Blood, Bread, and Roses*. A primal ancestress is crouched, animal-like, in seclusion, hiding from the wolf and the jackal. She contemplates the red blood coming from between her legs and knows that she must protect herself from bloodthirsty predators. Women are vulnerable.

With the advent of culture and ritualized protection came taboo. Menstruation taboos are among the oldest in the history of the world. From primal ancestress to lipstick lesbian, fashion and blood rites have fashioned the course of human life. Cosmetic, says Grahn, is related to cosmos. Menstrual blood on the lips was the first cultural cosmetic. Tattoos, piercings, makeup, and menstrual blood itself were used in menstrual rites and are still used to express rites of passage, markings of identity, sexual readiness, and warnings against coming too close.

The female power to bleed has held a paradoxical fascination, establishing a love/fear relationship between the sexes, for millennia. In her ground-breaking essay, "The Vampire Lovers," Andrea Weiss resurrects the woman of blood in the icon of the lesbian vampire. For patriarchal society, the lesbian poses a double threat, both as a woman, and as a woman with autonomous power. According to Weiss, the most prevalent image of the lesbian on screen, in six decades of Hollywood filmmaking, has been the image of the lesbian as a vampire.

Through the role of vampire, a woman comes to represent death. Through her seduction of other women, lesbianism becomes equated with pathological eroticism. One passionate love bite from another woman can transform a girl forever, into a ghoul. According to the thesis, lesbianism and the vampire's thirst for blood becomes a twisted double fear of menstruation and sexual power divorced from male control. For lesbians, this becomes an utterly campy profession of female power. Lesbian readers, undaunted by the fear of homoeroticism and female sexual prowess, can take an ironic distance and are easily able to invert the text for the perverse pleasure of laughing at the exaggerated fears of themselves.

Lesbianism, like vampirism, is eternal, passed on seductively from one woman to another. This notion of lesbian vampirism is taken over the top by Pat Califia in her essay "Slipping." Here she literally and graphically reappropriates this taboo act of eroticism. Blood lust of woman for woman becomes the transgressive forbidden desire flaunted as a lesbian sexual prerogative. But the blood of passion is also infused with the fear of death. Califia speaks frankly about AIDS and the high risk stakes associated with radical sex practices.

The image of the lesbian vampire on the screen was, for the most part, an image of an irresistible, seductive femme. As Andrea Weiss' essay explains, this image proved to be both titillating and a disturbing phenomenon for the male spectator. The femme vampire "appears 'normal' by society's standards for women, and yet is not."

Lest we leave the notion of "normal" sitting in the seats and in the eyes and minds of a male spectatorship, it's time to turn to the reappropriation of lesbian images on-screen for ourselves.

Jenni Olson's essay, "Butch Icons of the Silver Screen" shows us a myriad of desirable female butch images appropriated by a lesbian spectatorship from the world of film. This is, of course, is not to say that lesbians don't like femmes—far from it. But many dykes prefer to see butchy girls and manly women. Hollywood and independent filmmakers have produced their share of on-screen butches, some identifiable as lesbians.

Olson parades the cast of characters before us, from

tomboys to girls playing boys, to women as men who become women, to crossdressers, to cyberdykes. At the end of this essay is a wonderful filmography which may send you running to the video store, or, if Jenni has her way, you might consider starting a queer film festival in your own hometown.

My essay, "Chic by Nature," continues the lively exploration of genderfuck by foregrounding lesbian transgenderism. It exposes internal and external dynamics of role-playing. Scenes switch from segment to segment and different questions are raised about the shifting, intertwining, and oppositional paradigms of gender and race relations within lesbian/gay and mainstream culture. Overall, it is about the quest for love and community in a transitory world of ever-changing possibilities.

Judith Halberstam's "F2M: The Making of Female Masculinity," revamps the entire concept of femaleness. This fascinating essay calls for new sexual vocabularies that acknowledge sexualities and genders as styles—as fictions, rather than as fixed identities. Halberstam takes us on a mind-expanding romp through the queer world of genderbending ideologies and sexual expressions. She explains what is postmodern about lesbian identity and discusses cosmetic surgery and surgical reconstruction as it affects the entire nature vs. culture, biology as/not gender controversy. She quotes Judith Butler: "some girls like their boys to be girls," and then goes on to show how lovers read each other.

Eileen Myles, lesbian write-in candidate for U.S. President in 1992, writes about her media experiences, pop culture, the campaign trail, and her life as a lesbian video star. In her own boisterous, amusing and inimitable style, she takes on MTV, traditional family values, pro-lifers, and Madonna in "Campaign Diaries."

Part Two: Personal Reflections alters the point of view and switches the focus from media, gender theory and cultural representation, to autobiography and the non-fiction we write about ourselves and how we live our lesbian lives.

Dorothy Allison's keen personal observations about lesbian literature and her development as a writer are the subject of "Believing in Literature." Throughout the history of Western literature, our presence has been vilified, systematically usurped and denied. Allison believes that literature can change the world, and that it is imperative for lesbians to publish a literature that is truthful, meaningful and inspiring.

Like many of us who began writing at a time when undisguised lesbian subject matter was verboten, Allison didn't believe that she'd be able to say what she wanted and also make money through her writing. And, mind you, this is someone who recently had a blockbuster hit, receiving a National Book Award nomination for a first novel, *Bastard Out of Carolina*. Before *Bastard* Allison says that she was flat broke, sick and exhausted from years of activism, unpaid labor, and marginal employment. Regardless of the ins and outs of publishing, the vision of a lesbian literature is indomitable. Dorothy Allison writes, "I knew that what I wanted to do as a lesbian and feminist writer was to remake the world into a place where the truth would be hallowed, not held in contempt, where silence would be impossible."

Jewelle Gomez continues in this vein with her essay, "Because Silence Is Costly." Her history of Black lesbian/gay literature starts with the difficulty of the coming-out process. Gomez writes, "Coming out is not merely announcing a personal choice to the world; it is a step in accepting your identity. For Black lesbians/gays it means saying both I am gay and also declaring I am still Black." She analyzes the social and political ramifications around this dilemma. She ends up arguing that, despite its current falling out of favor with the commercial lesbian and gay community, the coming-out story may prove to be the most engaging aspect of the autobiographical form.

In her book, *The Apparitional Lesbian*, Terry Castle writes about "ghosting," whereby lesbian contributors to culture have been suppressed, ignored, censored or destroyed. She proceeds to resurrect the spectral lesbian subject as a vital mover and shaker in the history of culture and the arts. "Lesbians," she writes, "have made contributions to culture out of all proportion to their actual number."

In her autobiographical story "First Ed," Terry Castle "outs" herself in print—giving up the ghost. "First Ed" is a beautiful, lyrical essay about her first stirring for a dapper butch at the YWCA. The essay illustrates how early attractions can manifest years later as validated lesbian eroticism.

The piece called "South Side" is written as a scene from a longer script by San Francisco writer Camille Roy. Ostensibly it's about growing up on Chicago's South Side. The scene is a postmodern dialogic encounter between two lovers—Lover X and Lover Y. As with couples who know each other well and can fill in each others' stories, both lovers re-create the Monica narrative. The overtext tells of a young interracial lesbian relationship in a border neighborhood. A parallel dramatic line runs through the play, a commentary on boundaries and power dynamics, the tensions between competition and agreement, collaboration and aggression.

Sibling aggression and family power dynamics come up in Canyon Sam's autobiographical story "1975: All That Shattered." The poignant story of a dysfunctional Chinese-American family is told from the mother's elusive perspective. For the daughter, it's a look back at her coming-of-age and coming-out in the hippie days of Haight-Ashbury and lesbian feminist land collectives.

In "What Can We Make With Fire: What Stories, What Lives?" Robin Podolsky demonstrates that our art is made through our storytelling, which in turn creates our reality, and this is what makes us who we are. Our identity is fluid, and our stories break through boundaries, shattering contexts and self-identities that have lost their usefulness. Between her theoretical reflections, Podolsky tells her own stories; touching and moving personal narratives about race, about friends with AIDS, about positioning "queerness" both as a reflection and rejection of cultural attitudes.

Podolsky concedes: "Sure, history is a fiction, that means if we don't retell our own stories, we'll be trapped in the master narrative." She asks the question, one which was similarly posed in "Chic by Nature": how far can we go toward disassembling our own constructions, while those of heterosexuality remain largely intact? Her solution is clever: "We will loot the dominant culture for our aesthetic pleasure...destabilizing masculine and feminine while getting off on being both." And no, she admits, we are not perfect: "We've been known to lie to each other, slap our girlfriends, waste years on alcohol or the illusion of safety."

As she says, our stories need to be told. Our stories are our legacies. We create our own descendants. And we won't allow ourselves to be lost again.

In the closing and controversial essay, "Slipping," Pat

Califia talks about sex. Sex, she says, has always been a life-threatening, high-risk activity. But because of the pill and penicillin, we forgot that for a while. She read about the first lesbian case of AIDS in December of 1986 and chides the lesbian community for its unstated but widely held opinion that real lesbians don't get AIDS—only junkies and women who have sex with men are at risk.

Her point is well taken. Sex and passion have always been risky activities. Life has never been safe or disease-free, except maybe for vampires, or for goddesses.

Ending where we began, here's a thoughtful quotation from *Blood, Bread and Roses*: "Like our distant cousin apes, we are in and out of 'heat' or estrus, throughout the year, rather than undergoing one period of rut in the fall as the bear and deer do, or two or three periods of estrus as mice, dogs, and cats do. Sexual connection is thus constant and keeps our species in face-to-face tension all year round."

—San Francisco, 1994

PART ONE:

# How We Look,
# How We're Seen,
# How We Are

JUDY GRAHN
# How Menstruation
# Fashioned the Human Body

*Click. Click. Click. Click. Dark Chicago evening in 1946. I am six and at the window, listening to the shoes of passersby, waiting for the distinctive click of my sister's high heels on the sidewalk. Why does she wear such strange tall shoes? No one can answer, just as they cannot say why she puts bright red paint from a tube on her lips and black and lavender colors around her eyes. No one can explain why it takes my brother ten minutes to get dressed while it takes my sister an hour and a half. She must wash and roll her hair, then brush and pin it. She must pluck out some of her eyebrows, shave her legs and underarms. She must bathe and powder, and apply lotions and creams, greases, and colors. Her nails must be shaped and sharp and painted very red. Then selection of a dress: this one or that one, depending on her feelings and the occasion and the season and the time of day. Then her legs must be encased in stockings, the new sheer nylon ones that are so different from my mother's photos of her own legs in thick cotton stockings, white or black. Then come bracelets, earrings, a string of imitation pearls. Then the strange tall heels, gloves, a hat with a wide brim in summer, no brim in winter, a tiny veil on Sundays.*

*My father and brother make fun of how long it takes her to do all of this, how much of her salary she spends on it. But she doesn't care! She does what all her girlfriends do. She does it, my mother says, because she's a woman. But why does she do these particular things, over and over, so carefully? Why would women decide to do all this elaborate dressing, while our primate cousins do none of it? Perhaps because, my father says, we have no fur and need to keep warm. But my sister wears thin high heels and sheer stockings in the Chicago winter, and so his answer, acquired in a round-about way from Darwin, is shaky. It doesn't address the specifics, the strangeness of the rituals themselves, which I know baffle him as well.*

The ancestress has answers. Crouched in seclusion from the wolf or jackal, she contemplates the sticky red blood that is the cause of her dilemma. She comes to understand that she is both vulnerable and dangerous. She fashions her body, and in the process, she fashions the course of human life.

### Seclusion Rites and Body Language

A woman's relation to her whole body was regulated by menstrual law in the seclusion rites—her relationships to sex, to food, to how she held her body, how she slept, how she sat, how she walked, how she kept her skin and hair, and what she might or might not touch. At the end of seclusion, which for menarche often ended at first light, the menstruant was frequently carried, by a group of women of her family, to water. In the river, lake, or stream, she was washed. Then her hair was meticulously cared for, washed and oiled, combed and braided, dyed and decorated. Her whole body was painted and bedecked with all the finery her family could afford and that her culture found meaningful. Then, a creature of more dazzling display than any other human in the tribe's experience, she emerged from "the shade" into public celebration, dancing and feasting. At some time after these rites of body—in some cases, hours, and in others, years, she married and took her adult position.

"Cosmetic" is related to "cosmos," entire ordered reality, and both are related to the Greek word *cosmetikos,* ordering of the world. Of other related terms, "cosmology" refers to astronomical study of space-time relationships, and also to a branch of world-describing metaphysics. "Cosmogony" means a description of the origin of the universe, and "cosmography" means a (written) description of the order of nature. These are definitions that apply very nicely to narrative metaform, human culture after writing and storytelling have developed. But origin mythology specifies times before speech, before drawing and writing, theater or song. To get back that far, I want to use *cosmetikos* to refer to the use of body arts to enact a world origin story, or cosmogony.

In the course of their rites, women took complete charge of the body, shaping it, carving it, decorating it, restraining it, and displaying it with conscious intent to express and instruct in the principles of cosmogony. The body arts are thus metaforms, enactments and physical embodiments of ideas that developed through perception of the connection of menstruation to outside events both terrible and wonderful, and to the lunar cycle and other natural phenomena. The cosmeticians were originally the menstruant's mother, grandmother, aunts, and sisters, joined later by her brothers and husband. From the beginning, the cosmeticians who decorated her for her emergence from seclusion were expressing an ordering of the world; they were, literally, fashioning it.

Their fashioning of themselves was a way of telling what they knew. As the Dogon people say it, "a woman without adornment is speechless." The adornment itself is speech.[1] Not only the adornment, but the flesh itself speaks, for a decorated woman's body is not just that of a shaved animal in earrings. Her stance and gesture, her shape and manner, her inner controls and releases are all reflections of the time spent in her various seclusions and beautification rites of emergence, with their special meanings of human safety, origination, and attraction.

The body arts of *cosmetikos* continued the principle of creation through separation. The earliest separations involved the removal of the menstruant's physical person from the general population during menstruation. She was shut "away" from everyday life, in the bush, the forest, in the darkest part of the dwellings. Her body became the focus of intense scrutiny from the time that she began to comprehend its measurement and to instruct others in its dimensions. Her body was dangerous and powerful, so that everyone had to know where she was during her dangerous time. The men must not look at her in her numinous phase, lest they die, and lest Chaos close around human consciousness. They must have been keenly aware at all times that she was in seclusion. Warned sharply away from certain areas by their mothers and sisters, the men learned to be ever-vigilant in the presence of the woman. To watch her, and to watch out for her.

Emphasis was put on the power of her eyes: she must not see light, men, bodies of water, or in many cases, anything at all for a specified period of time. She must keep her head lowered and use her gaze carefully, strategically, for she had the eye of death as well as of life. Emphasis was put on her mouth; by extension, it represented her bleeding vagina, as indeed did all the openings of her body. Emphasis was put on all moisture from her body. Not only the various bloods, but milk, tears, mucus and spit, urine and vulva fluids became endowed with special powers. Emphasis was put on her skin, hair, and body hair, analogous to the surface of the earth with its trees, bushy plants, and flowing streams.

Emphasis was put on her hands, too dangerous at times to touch anything at all, yet entrusted with the newborn and with the gathering and preparation of most of the food eaten by her family. Emphasis was put on her feet, that they not touch the fragile earth inappropriately. And emphasis was put on her breasts and pelvis, for after her taboos were used to repel possible mates, to turn their faces from her, she had to entice male attention back to her person in order to engage with them. She had to ensure their safety in approaching her. She was completely repellent one day and completely attractive the next; she was paradox itself.

The motives for body decoration and reshaping, then, have at base been religious, from re-ligio: re-binding, re-connection. Women needed to reconnect with men and children. Their decorations expressed human connections to each other, as well as to the world outside the human body. Moreover, decoration expressed the gradually increasing abilities, brought about by menstrual use of metaform, of prediction and memory.

## Cosmetics: Blood Signals and Paint

*Cosmetikos* began as simple signals of warning and instruction, enabling women to control how they were seen, whether they were avoided or approached. The woman didn't need to display her vulva, she could paint her mouth with menstrual blood—and, in doing so, she created body painting. Plain menstrual blood is still used as a signal in India, where "the condition of a menstruating woman is indicated by her wearing round her neck a handkerchief stained with menstrual blood."[2]

The teaching of menstrual principles to the men and the use of blood as a signal or sign of status was heightened by the use of slashing, with a thorn, flint, or fingernail. The women could create blood at will, through cutting. Australian tribal women danced during menstruation, and in a myth they cut their breasts, as if reveling in blood powers.[3] The sight of blood on another woman's thigh could start a woman bleeding, so slashing, for some people, perhaps was a method of synchrony. Women found that they could have menstrual signals visible on their faces and other parts of their bodies even when they were not in the dangerous state of menstruation. Cuts around the mouth and other parts of the face or body displayed the ideas of menstrual blood and of the "wet" vulva. Through the act of cutting, women recreated the creative power, bringing warnings, protection, repellence, attraction, and religious signification. The blood signals marked the young menstruant as having passed into the station of a fertile, fully powerful, and world-forming woman.

The mouth was made into a parallel signal for vulva by coloring and marking it to look as though it was bleeding. Lips have been emphasized in many parts of the world by lip tattoos, a thin line drawn with a thorn or flint around the outside or directly on the lips and rubbed with pigment. One rite in particular, the permanent marking of the chin with vertical lines, was practiced on girls at menarche in diverse regions of the world. The chin tattoo is very suggestive of a bleeding mouth and avoids having to make the slash repeatedly to signal menstruation. Chin tattooing was typically done with three vertical lines that ran from the lower lip to the bottom of the chin, two at the corners of the mouth and one in the center. These were usually straight lines, though sometimes they were zigzag or a line of dots.

The reason given for menarchal chin tattoos of Karoks and others was "so she won't look like a man." Among native tribes of the West Coast, chin tattooing was primarily a mark of the female status achieved at menarche. Though men were often also tattooed on the face, including three lines on the chin, usually their tattoos were more generalized. Among the Maori, for instance, men were tattooed all over the face while women retained the specific vertical lines on the chin and outlining the lips. Among some people, tattooed lines continued down the neck onto the breasts or stomach. Blood overflowing from the mouth would follow a similar course, and chin tattoos were sometimes called "dribble lines."

After learning to use the original substance of blood as a

signal, women used the principle of metaform to replace blood with other red substances. They especially used the iron-rich powder ocher and red clays, though any reddish substance that could make a red dye seems to have caught female attention. Metaformically, the paint was the menstruation of the earth. In Australia, "the deposits of red ocher...are said by Aborigines to have been caused by the flow of blood from women's vulvas in the most ancient times which they call Alcheringa."[4] Australian, Hottentot, and Bushmen tribes evidently all associated ceremonial red paint with menstrual blood, the Australians saying the paint was "really" women's blood. Typically, the paint was red ocher mixed with grease. Then white chalk and black, blue and gold, and other pigments also came to be used as body paint. Men adapted them to their parallel menstrual rites.

Lipstick, then, may be considered the first cosmetic: "Among the Dieri and other Australian tribes, menstruating women were marked with red paint round the mouth, while among the tribes of Victoria a menstruating woman is painted red from the waist up. Among Tapuga tribes of Brazil and on the Gold Coast of Africa, she is also painted red."[5] Among the Cheyenne, at her first menstruation a girl was painted red all over her body and secluded for four days in a special little lodge.[6] In China, formerly, a woman customarily put a red mark in the middle of her forehead to signal that she was menstruating, and also as a cosmetic.[7]

Pregnancy, childbirth, and nursing were also special states designated with red paint. The Kaffir and many other tribal women painted their bodies with red ocher when they were pregnant. Pregnancy and childbirth are numinous phases of life, but it was because of the creative/decreative powers specifically accruing to women's blood that the use of red signaling during pregnancy and lactation gave women enormous powers of restraint over men and the spacing of childbearing. In some tribes, by using paint women might signal "no sex" for six or seven years at a time, while they continued nursing.[8] More usual was the period of three years used by Nigerian women of the eighteenth century, who kept their bodies smeared with red earth throughout the entire period as a public announcement that they were bearing, nursing, or weaning a child.[9]

One meaning of the blood signals was surely reassurance: "It's safe to look at me now," or "I'm old enough to bleed, but I'm not doing it right now," or "Now I'm available for sex or marriage." Among other peoples, the red marks meant danger, keep away, not sexually available at this time: "Don't look at me." Mouth marking and paint was a display not only of the female power to bleed, but of a range of complex signals meaning "come here" or "stay away."

All the earliest cosmetics—menstrual blood, slashed blood, and tattoos of blue or red lines suggestive of blood on the face—must have enabled women to free themselves from some of the severest world-forming taboos. Most of the complex taboos would have remained intact in the initial major rite of menarche, but more minor ones would mark all the menstrual periods after the first. Western reporters noticed that the strict seclusions of the menstruant were being replaced in the nineteenth century by milder menstrual signals, such as a brightly colored scarf, face paint, a special apron or ring, or even a smoking pipe clenched in her teeth.[10]

Whole peoples in older times studied the color red through body use. Some completely painted their bodies red (the

"Red Clay People" of the eastern United States). They tattooed themselves from head to foot (Scotland, Canada, Borneo). They plastered their hair with ocher and grease, with thick red clay (South America, Africa), or stained their teeth red (Southeast Asia, South Pacific, South America), or painted and dyed their hair, hands, and feet with henna (India, Middle East, North Africa, Europe). Even now, when menstrual rite has largely vanished, women continue to paint their cheeks and lips red to impart vitality, health, sexual desirability, and self-respect.

## Other Techniques of Menstrual Display

In addition to using tattoos and paint for ritual purposes, people marked their mouths and bodies with bits of special carved wood and shell. Typically, these "plugs" were either slender and pinlike or round and buttonlike. They were pushed through holes punctured in the skin, ears, nose, septum, or embedded in the flesh of the menstruant. Like elaborate tattooing, the process of making a large hole in a girl's lower lip or ear might begin years before the onset of menstruation. Among the Tlingit or Kolosh Indians of Alaska, following a year of seclusion in a little hut or cage, the menstruant was given a feast "at which a slit was cut in her under lip parallel to the mouth, and a piece of wood or shell was inserted to keep the aperture open."[11]

The Jivaro woman of Peru and Ecuador formerly wore a long stick in her lower lip following menarche. Some South American men, those of the Karaja tribe, for example, also wore long lip pegs.[12]

In Africa, women's lip plugs developed elaborately, with round and trapezoidal shapes and a variety of materials and sizes. Although their original use has been forgotten, the round lip plugs, made of reddish wood or, in later days, of white ivory or a shining metal, resembled a display of the full moon or the sun. Some of these plugs were disks of various sizes; others were carved balls fitted with a flat base that was inserted into the lower lip. For heavy and large plugs, some women extracted their lower incisor teeth to make room for the base. Although the stretched lips healed, the initial operations were painful and risked infection, and the weight of the ornaments must have caused enormous strain on the facial muscles. Women in East Africa stretched their lips increasingly throughout their lives, inserting grooved plates as large as six inches in diameter.

The inserted plugs, pins, and plates drew attention to the mouth. They also protected it from "evil spirits," for it was widely believed that agents causing ill health or other disasters entered the body through its openings. All the openings of the face and head were, by extension, vaginas in need of protection. Thus, for the Dogon people, whose culture carefully balances gender imagery, the outer ear is the male genitalia and the inner ear the female. The inner ear might be protected by having a stick run through the top of the outer ear, or by hanging distracting objects from the earlobes. In any number of tribes, a woman might wear a long aluminum "stick," like a three-inch hatpin, through the top or back of her ear, or she might have a series of rings in a line up the outer ear—all to prevent evil spirits from entering that orifice.[13]

Rings and jewels are worn in the side of the nose in cultures around the world, and particularly in India. The nose is also pierced to hold a veil for the mouth. For example, a long loop through the septum may suspend a veil of dangling pieces that fall across the mouth.[14] Protective ornaments have also been embedded around—and between—the eyes.

Scarification was also used to adorn and protect. Dogon women display long decorative scars on their foreheads representing the fertile vulva, and these deep grooves are kept oiled so they will be "wet," a positive condition in their arid farmland. In many African tribes, *cosmetikos* consisted of a combination of embedded protective objects near the orifices and elaborate scar-ification using bars, dots, Vs, and other shapes pertaining to religious principles and the woman's tribe, family, and status. Her body was a writing tablet before writing, covered with information. Her breasts, abdomen, and back might be decoratively scarred as well. Sometimes smooth objects such as millet or rice were embedded all over a woman's upper body—planted in the earth of her skin—for a raised tattoo of great beauty and significance.

The meanings of *cosmetikos* evolved beyond its initial task of protecting the people from the harmful aspects of menstrual creation. On the California coast, among the Gabrielino tribe, tattooing began for girls at puberty, as we would expect. But the elaborate patterns comprised a variety of complex social meanings: "Before puberty, girls were tattooed on their foreheads and chins, while adult women had tattoos covering an area from their eyes down to their breasts. Men tattooed their foreheads with vertical and or horizontal lines."[15] These tattoos became a mark of distinct identity, defining ownership of land. "Some individuals owned real estate, and property boundaries were marked by painting a copy of the owner's personalized tattoo on trees, posts, and rocks. These marks were almost equivalent to the owner's name" and were known even to non-Gabrielinos.[16]

This method of designating land is reminiscent of the boundaries established by menstrual regulations elsewhere. In old Hawaii, for example, the plot of land surrounding the menstrual hut was declared off limits to the general population. It was in this ground that the women buried their menstrual pads."[17]

Tattooing may have enabled people to memorize and reproduce the specific markings of animals and fish, as an origin myth from the Marshall Islands suggests.[18] Though the cave drawings along the California coast are mostly attributed to men, it is also known that some were created by women who had just emerged from the seclusions of menarche.[19] From the ritual drawing on human skin, begun by a mother's outlining of her daughter's lips with a thorn, our ancestors may have moved onto other surfaces to express the mysteries they were learning.

### Fashioning of Body Shape

In addition to coloring and drawing on body surfaces, women consciously took charge of the shape of their whole bodies and gave them the cultural significance, the cosmological statements we call "beauty." At the conclusion of her menarchal rite, a woman's hair was carefully combed and shaped, its "flow" brought under control. The most essential metaphor of hair is liquidity, enhanced through grease and oil to make it shine. In arid areas of the world, where rainfall is treasured, the apparent wetness of the hair underscored the deeply held belief that menstruants assist or control the weather, attracting water and adding to the general fertility of the world. In areas of heavy rainfall, dry-looking hair would also serve to control the sky's vagaries. Hair is plastered with mud and ocher as well as oil; it is braided, cornrowed, tied, plaited, beaded, fluffed, straightened, curled, and shaped into all manner of significant patterns. For instance, women of one Mongolian tribe wore their hair in large horn shapes, held in place with metal and wood, to represent the fierce independent spirit of their herding people.

Control of the hair's wildness indicates control of menstrual flow. The coiffing of the hair—especially women's hair—symbolized the ordering of chaotic forces. This need for order has also provided a motive for depilation (pulling out or shaving hair), which is practiced worldwide.

Women shaped their bodies according to metaformic principles. Were the people nervous about famine? The menstruant emerged fattened, her mother and aunts having stuffed her for weeks with their richest foods, whether she consented or not.[20] Various peoples all around the world have, for differing reasons, considered fatness in women beautiful, and some took fattening to such extremes that the young women could not raise their bodies from the ground and needed help walking.[21]

Women mold their bodies for practical purposes. African women often wanted long breasts, in order to feed babies carried on their backs during long walks, and so at puberty they used "bands and ropes to compress the base of the breast and elongate it." Polynesians on the other hand admired firm breasts, and Samoan girls trained their breasts to point upward.[22] In the United States, both extremes prevail: athletic women make their breasts completely vanish, while film stars, models, and sex-club dancers enlarge theirs with diet and silicone implants.

Women mold their bodies for social purposes. In a materialist society, these purposes can be individual and psychological. I remember deciding, at sixteen, that I didn't want to attract sexual attention from men, so I decided to be very, very thin. I accomplished this through a diet of cigarettes, coffee, and not much food, stopping when my breasts and buttocks had virtually disappeared, and ignoring the persistent cough that kept me awake at night. Body shaping has long been dangerous: embedded jewelry can cause infections; extreme use of bracelets, leg, neck, and arm rings can cut off circulation, even cause crippling; breast implants can leak silicone into the surrounding tissue; diet drugs do all kinds of damage. Will we ever stop molding our appearance toward some purpose? I would argue that the motives behind *cosmetikos* are too deep-seated.

The menstruant uses *cosmetikos* to indicate how she has gone about protecting herself and her society from the dangers made conscious by menstrual synchroneity. Now that the woman has the Serpent, she understands her capacity to cause or prevent the Flood, and all her society understands that human actions have consequences. Emerging from the dark chaos of her seclusion, her metaformic paints, tattoos, scars, and embedded decorations indicate safety and allurement, group identification, order, and promise of peace and well-being. Her hard-won "beauty" embodies the cosmological understandings for all her people and ensures their survival in the unsteady, floating world. No wonder her community greeted her emergence at menarche with a joyful celebration and feast. She was *the way back*: the return from fear, danger, and decomposition to reassurance, renewal, and orderliness. They needed only to look at her to know who they were and how they were doing.

## Notes

1. Marcel Griaule, *Conversations with Ogotommêli* (London: International/African Institute/Oxford University Press, 1965) p. 82. In describing women's beauty, Ogotommêli said that "to be naked is to be without speech."

2. Robert Briffault, *The Mothers* (London: Macmillan, 1969) vol. 2, pp. 14–15.

3. Knight, *Blood Magic: The Anthropology of Menstruation,* ed. Buckley and Gottlieb (Berkeley: University of California Press, 1988) p. 237.

4. Evelyn Reed, *Woman's Evolution* (New York: Pathfinder Press, 1957) p. 98. See also Briffault, *The Mothers,* vol. 2, pp. 412–17: "Since woman's blood was taboo, daubing with blood became the mark or insignia of the tabooed condition. In the course of time red ocher came to serve as a substitute for blood."

5. Briffault, *The Mothers,* vol. 2, pp. 414–15.

6. Sir James George Frazer, *New Golden Bough* (New York: St. Martin's Press, 1966) p. 668.

7. Douglas and Slinger, *Sexual Secrets* (New York: Destiny Books, 1979) pp. 241, 352.

8. Briffault, *The Mothers,* vol. 2, pp. 390–96.

9. Reed, *Woman's Evolution,* pp. 135, 36.

10. Briffault, *The Mothers,* vol. 2, p. 397.

11. Frazer, *The Golden Bough* (1929), vol. 2, p. 600.

12. Ger Daniëls, ed., *Folk Jewelry of the World* (New York: Rizzoli, 1989) p. 32.

13. Angela Fisher, *Africa Adorned* (New York: Harry Abrams, 1984) p. 137. The Dogon balance of gender and the body is in Griaule, *Conversations with Ogotommêli.*

14. Daniels, *Folk Jewelry of the World,* p. 84.

15. Robert Heizer, *Handbook of North American Indians* (Washington, D.C.: Smithsonian Press, 1978) vol. 8, p. 540.

16. Ibid.

17. Handy and Pukui, *The Polynesian Family System in Ka-'u Hawaii,* (Rutland: Charles Tuttle, 1972) pp. 10–11.

18. Barbara Sproul, ed., *Primal Myths: Creation Myths Around the World* (San Francisco: Harper & Row, 1991) p. 334. In the male origin story cited by Sproul, the god Lowa sent two men to tattoo everything in the world, and this is how each kind of animal got its characteristic markings.

19. Heizer, *Handbook of North American Indians*, vol. 8, p. 688. Rock painting was explicitly included in menarchal rites of the Luiseno (p. 556).

20. Briffault, *The Mothers*, vol. 2, pp. 162–163. Briffault says the young Tuareg women protested vehemently, to no avail.

21. Ibid.

22. Ibid.

## ANDREA WEISS
# The Vampire Lovers

Lesbians are sharks, vampires, creatures from the deep lagoon, godzillas, hydrogen bombs, inventions of the laboratory, werewolves—all of whom stalk Beverly Hills by night. Christopher Lee, in drag, in the Hammer Films, middle period, is my ideal lesbian.
— Bertha Harris "What Is a Lesbian?"[1]

Dracula, that tall, dark, handsome menace, has been given some stiff competition over the years by an even more attractive female counterpart—the lesbian vampire. She has found an enthusiastic medium for visual expression in the cinema, which has resurrected lesbian vampire tales dating far back in literature and legend.

Merging two kinds of sexual outlaws, the lesbian vampire is more than simply a negative stereotype. She is a complex and ambiguous figure, at once an image of death and an object of desire, drawing on profound subconscious fears that the living have toward the dead and that men have toward women, while serving as a focus for repressed fantasies. The generic vampire image both expresses and represses sexuality, but the lesbian vampire especially operates in the sexual rather than the supernatural realm.

The English-language films considered here are but a

small sampling of the many horror films that feature female vampires with lesbian tendencies. The scope and persistence of this phenomenon should not be underestimated; outside of male pornography, the lesbian vampire is the most persistent lesbian image in the history of the cinema. The lesbian vampire films cover six decades of film history, from the 1930s to the 1980s; their countries of origin include the United States, Great Britain, France, West Germany, Belgium, Spain, and Italy. The European films, with such titles as *Vampyros Lesbos—Die Erbin des Dracula* (Jess Franco, Germany/Spain, 1971) and *La Novia Ensangrentada* or *The Blood-Spattered Bride* (Aranda, Spain, 1972), sound enticing, yet must await further study.

In the early 1960s, Barbara Steele played a vampire in a number of Italian films with lesbian overtones, including *Black Sunday* (Mario Bava, 1960), a film which influenced the screenwriters of the English lesbian vampire films produced a decade later, and *Castle of Blood* or *La Danza Macabra* (Antonio Margheriti, 1963), in which Steele's character kills her lesbian cousin and lover (Margaret Robsham). Jean Rollin directed a series of surrealist French horror films, including *Le Viol du Vampire* (1967), *La Vampire Nue* (1969), *Le Frisson des Vampires* (1970), and *Vierges et Vampires* (1971), all of which sacrificed narrative coherence for shocking sadomasochistic lesbian images. Rollin's iconography features leather and metal chains, spikes protruding from women's breasts, scenes of gang rape, and vampires reduced to drinking from their own veins.

Such jarring imagery departs significantly from that of the typical, more romantic lesbian vampire film, which has certain fairly consistent characteristics: Gothic themes and imagery, large empty castles and dark, romantic landscapes, and the arrival, early in the film, of a mysterious aristocratic figure. With a few exceptions, these horror films were made on very small budgets, with extremely low production values. Their low-budget look gives them an exaggerated, camp quality which, for viewers today, is often their redeeming feature. They were originally shown in second-rate commercial movie houses or in drive-in theaters, and now a number of them have been resurrected on the home-video market.

The association of vampirism with lesbianism is far-reaching and long-lived. As Richard Dyer has pointed out, the literary images of each are closely related and often described in the same morbid language.[2] For example, in the 1915 novel, *Regiment of Women* by Winifred Ashton (pseud. Clemence Dane), the following description is not of a vampire's victim, but of one woman who has fallen in love with another: "So thin—she's growing so dreadfully thin. Her neck! You should see her neck—salt-cellars, literally! And she had such a beautiful neck!... And so white and listless."

The connection between lesbians and vampires has not been restricted to the horror genre, but resonates throughout much of the existing cultural representations of lesbianism. In a number of European art films of the 1960s and 1970s, such as Ingmar Bergman's *Persona* (Sweden, 1965) and Rainer Werner Fassbinder's *The Bitter Tears of Petra von Kant* (West Germany, 1972), vampirism is suggested through the erotic relationship between two women, in which one woman takes over the personality or soul of the other. Susan Sontag has described the elusive plot of *Persona* as "two women bound together in a passionate agonized relationship which is rendered mythically as vampirism: at one point, Alma sucks Elizabeth's blood."[3]

In *Surpassing the Love of Men,* Lillian Faderman finds that a spate of lesbian vampire novels appeared in the first half of the twentieth century. Vampire imagery serves as a metaphor for lesbianism in such books as Francis Brett Young's *White Ladies* (1935) and Dorothy Baker's *Trio* (1943), and *Vampir* (1932), which was published in Germany under the anagram Ano Nymous. Faderman connects the emergence of lesbianism as vampirism to the pathologizing of women's relationships by medical and cultural authorities. The vampire metaphor, Faderman asserts, served to enforce the transition from nineteenth-century socially accepted close female relationships to the redefinition of such relationships as deviant in the first half of the twentieth century.[4]

Although the lesbian vampire image resurfaced in this period, its origins can be traced back to several earlier sources of vampire lore. The most significant of these is the Victorian novel *Carmilla* (1871) by J. Sheridan Le Fanu, which predates Bram Stoker's *Dracula* by twenty-five years. The fictional Carmilla is an aristocratic noblewoman, the Countess Millarca Karnstein, who reappears as a vampire one hundred fifty years after her physical death. It is a typical Victorian novel: genteel on the surface, but beneath is the darker side of the spirit. Laura, Carmilla's "victim," describes her vampire lover in romantic terms:

> [Carmilla] used to place her pretty arms around my neck, draw me to her, and laying her cheek next to mine, murmur with her lips near my ear, "Dearest, your little heart is wounded; think me not cruel because I obey the irresistible law of my strength and weakness; if your dear heart is wounded, my wild heart bleeds with yours."

Carmilla falls in love with her so-called victims; she is char-
acterized sympathetically in that she acts out of compulsion
rather than malice. Gene Damon, writing in the early American lesbian publication *The Ladder,* claimed that the novel
*Carmilla* has "long been a sub-basement Lesbian classic" but
the film based on it, *The Vampire Lovers,* is "a male movie,
for a male audience."[5] What has survived of *Carmilla* from
Victorian literature and worked its way into twentieth-century cinema is its muted expression of lesbianism: no longer
sympathetically portrayed, but now reworked into a male
pornographic fantasy.

Although in the earliest lesbian vampire film, *Dracula's
Daughter* (Lambert Hillyer, 1936), the sexuality of the vampire (Gloria Holden) is discreetly implied, by the late 1960s
and early 1970s, lesbian sexual behavior had become graphically depicted, another titillating, exaggerated characteristic
of the excessive B-movie genre. One obvious explanation for
this change in representation is the gradual relaxation of the
strict censorship laws in the United States and Great Britain
in the mid-1960s, which these films further encouraged.
No longer hunted by censors, some twenty or more lesbian
vampires could be found stalking the silver screen between
the years of 1970 and 1974 alone. In the early 1970s, Hammer
Studios in Great Britain released its trilogy of X-rated "sex-
ploitation flicks": *The Vampire* Lovers (Roy Baker, 1970),
*Twins of Evil* (John Hough, 1971) and *Lust for a Vampire*
(Jimmy Sangster, 1971). *The Vampire Lovers* establishes
the narrative formula that subsequent films, with slight
deviations, take up, and helps define the genre by fully
exploiting the pornographic value of the relationship
between the vampire and her victim.

This pornographic appeal was a strong motivation for

producing most of these films in the first place. Tudor Gates, the screenwriter of the Hammer trilogy, claims that with these films Hammer was deliberately challenging the British Board of Film Censors on the question of where to draw the line on allowable representation.[6] By the early 1970s, graphic sexual images that elsewhere would be excised by censors was considered more acceptable within the realm of the supernatural. As the 1970s wore on, these images became increasingly possible in other forms of cinema, and the lesbian vampire was no longer necessary to circumvent censorship regulations. Still, the figure didn't completely disappear; she continued to hold an erotic power and fascination beyond her purely pornographic value. Although on the decline since the mid-1970s, it is in her nature to return again.

The Hammer films are invariably set in an ambiguous, mythologized past, when strict gender roles demanded that men be brave and women helpless. Yet the films' production unmistakably belongs to the late 1960s and early 1970s, a period in which such clear-cut definitions of masculinity and femininity were increasingly coming under fire. Bonnie Zimmerman, writing in *Jump Cut* (1981), speculates on the relationship between the sudden appeal of the lesbian vampire in 1970 and the initial gains of the feminist movement:

Although direct parallels between social forces and popular culture are risky at best, the popularity of the lesbian vampire film in the early 1970s may be related to the beginnings of an international feminist movement.... Since feminism between 1970 and 1973 was not yet perceived as a fundamental threat, men could enjoy the sexual thrill provided by images of lesbian vampires stealing women and sometimes destroying men in the process. The creators of those images—like the pornographic filmmakers who appeal to male fantasies with scenes of lesbianism—must have felt secure enough in their power and that of their primarily male audience to flirt with lesbianism and female violence against men.[7]

But a reconsideration of this lesbian vampire popularity more strongly suggests that what the creators of these images must have felt secure about was not so much their male power as the potential box-office returns on a low-budget exploitation product. It was, in fact, the huge financial success of *The Vampire Lovers* that motivated Hammer Films to continue with their lesbian theme. The relationship which Zimmerman seeks to establish between the early 1970s feminist movement and the appearance of so many lesbian vampire films rests not on the security but on the insecurity that the feminist movement generated in male spectators at that time. Feminists were angrily demanding sexual autonomy from men and control over their own bodies. Strengthened by participation in consciousness-raising groups, many women across the United States and in Europe demanded sexual pleasure and sexual equality with their husbands and boyfriends, and many more left these men and proclaimed their lesbianism. Under such circumstances, men understandably felt their dominant social position to be dangerously threatened.

Although psychic fears and historical circumstances rarely coincide so directly or neatly, and it would be reductive to explain the former as solely the product of the latter, the emergence of the lesbian vampire in this period does, in some measure, symbolize this threat. The lesbian vampire provokes and articulates anxieties in the heterosexual male spectator, only for the film to quell these anxieties and reaffirm his maleness through the vampire's ultimate destruction.

The lesbian vampire is at once attractive and threatening to men, in part because she expresses an active sexual desire, something which men may fantasize about safely in the cinema even while threatened by its prospect at home.

While sexually active, the lesbian vampire is still visually coded as feminine: she has long hair, large breasts, pale white skin, and wears floor-length, translucent dresses. Unlike the "masculine" images of lesbians in more mainstream films of the late sixties and early seventies like *The Fox* (Mark Rydell, 1966) and *The Killing of Sister George* (Robert Aldrich, 1968), the lesbian vampire fits the stereotype, not of the mannish lesbian, but of the white, feminine, heterosexual woman. Her vampirism, therefore, is doubly disturbing, as she appears "normal" by society's standards for women, and yet is not. James Donald has noted that "works of the fantastic insist upon the delusory nature of perception" and "play...upon the insecurity of the boundaries between the 'I' and the 'not-I.'"[8] The vampire's femininity contributes to this insecurity by her ability to "pass" as heterosexual; she is not visually identifiable as either lesbian or vampire.

The lesbian vampire not only crosses boundaries (through passing), but breaks down boundaries between the male "I" and the female "not-I" as well. While appearing to be excessively "feminine," she also contradicts and confounds this femininity through the anxious attention focused on her mouth. Christopher Craft's illuminating study of Bram Stoker's *Dracula* describes the vampire's mouth:

> As the primary site of erotic experience...this mouth equivocates, giving the lie to the easy separation of the masculine and the feminine. Luring at first with an inviting orifice, a promise of red softness, but delivering instead a piercing

bone, the vampire mouth fuses and confuses...the gender-based categories of the penetrating and the receptive. With its soft flesh barred by hard bone, its red crossed by white, this mouth compels opposites and contrasts into a frightening unity.[9]

Medical case histories of the early twentieth century reveal deep anxieties about the possibility of female penetration. Ridiculously imposing a heterosexual model of sexual behavior onto lesbian desire, medical "experts" actually attempted to measure imagined "deformity" of lesbians' genitalia and their possibilities for sexual penetration.[10] In the lesbian vampire story, this anxiety has been displaced and refocused on the mouth, another "feminine" sexual orifice which combines the "masculine" ability to penetrate, via the teeth. Thus the vampire embodies age-old popular fears of women which have been expressed through the image of the "vagina dentata," the vagina with teeth, the penetrating woman. Jean Rollin's lesbian vampire with spikes protruding from her breasts expresses a similar anxiety.

The fluctuations between desire and fear generated by the vampire seem to require a "strict, indeed almost schematic formal management of narrative material," as Christopher Craft has demonstrated.[11] This management of narrative material is formulaic: the vampire is first introduced in order to disrupt and invert the "natural order" and to provoke anxieties in the characters and spectator alike; the vampire then engages in vampirism as entertainment and sexual titillation for the prolonged middle section of the narrative; and finally the vampire is destroyed and the "natural order" reaffirmed. In the case of the lesbian vampire, a more specific narrative formula is often further imposed upon the generic vampire plot: a lesbian vampire and a mortal man compete for the possession of a woman. In this bisexual triangle, the man is aligned with the forces of good, the vampire with the forces of evil, and the woman whose fate hangs in the balance is usually a "nice, sweet girl" with no intrinsic moral value attached to her but who is merely a receptacle to assume the values of either one.

This alignment of moral values with specific characters is established at the start. In the Hammer Films production, *The Vampire Lovers,* the man is shown in relationship to church, family, and community; Carmilla (Ingrid Pitt) is a stranger with a "foreign" accent, a newcomer with no community ties. While the man is a moral, proper gentleman and rides a white horse, the vampire is clearly a "bad girl." It is this "bad girl," however, who holds the stronger appeal. Linda Williams has pointed out that "it is a truism of the horror genre that sexual interest resides most often in the monster [or vampire] and not in the bland ostensible heroes...who often prove powerless at the crucial moment."[12] Carmilla's "bad-ness" is conveyed through sexual signs: her dress is low-cut, her smile mischievous and seductive, and her body too well developed to confirm the youthful, girlish pose she assumes. The victim, Emma (Madeleine Smith), over whom they compete, is younger, starry-eyed and innocent, and, at least initially, subservient to her father.

While it may be possible for lesbian viewers to derive some pleasure from the vampire's sexual escapades, these scenes invariably cater to male heterosexual fantasy. One particularly explicit scene from *The Vampire Lovers* is a perfect example of male voyeurism and, ultimately, male sadistic impulses. Emma comes into Carmilla's bedroom while Carmilla is taking a bath. First we see Carmilla in a medium shot, eyes averted offscreen and naked from the waist up in the bathtub. Her large breasts are center screen and dominate the shot. Then she turns as she rises, and we have a view of her entire torso from the back just as she drapes a towel around her. These two shots underscore the spectator's position as voyeur: able to see her body but fleetingly, before she covers herself, and without meeting her gaze. Carmilla walks to the mirror and sits so that her back is to the camera; we simultaneously see her naked back and, in the mirror reflection, her face, neck, shoulders, and breasts. (The standard myth that vampires lack a reflection is dispensed with here in the service of prurient interests.) Thus, at the moment when the lesbian vampire is about to seduce her victim for the first time, her image is rendered less threatening: it is visually fragmented onto different spatial planes through the framing of the foreground and mirror images. This symbolic dismemberment of her body foreshadows her eventual destruction by the film's end.

In this bedroom scene, Carmilla tells Emma to borrow one of her dresses, but first to take off everything underneath. Emma's hesitancy, "What will my father say?" and Carmilla's reassurance, "He will enjoy it, as all men do," further speaks to the pleasures of the male spectator and establishes the context in which to view what follows. A half-naked Carmilla chases a half-naked Emma around the room, and they land conveniently on the bed. We see them embrace; and then, for a moment, a lamp in the foreground obstructs our view. This obstruction postpones voyeurism, which is a way of heightening and intensifying voyeuristic pleasure. The bulbous, symmetrical shape of the lamp at once shields our view of the women and symbolically re-creates the fetishized breast imagery in the foreground of the shot. Thus voyeurism and fetishism work together in this scene to contain and assuage the threat the vampire poses to the male spectator.

Within the narrative, the vampire represents the threat of violence as well as of sexuality. Usually the vampire seduces rather than attacks her victims; this can be seen as a relatively positive attribute in that the lesbian vampire doesn't seek to destroy her victims, but rather to make them into accomplices. Furthermore, seduction suggests a complicity on the part of the victim, indicating the relationship is mutually desirable to a certain extent. But lest we develop too much admiration for this charming seductress, random and gruesome violence is occasionally added to heighten the sense of perversion and destruction that she embodies. That this violence is often directed at women, for whom the vampire has a distinct sexual preference, serves further to link images of lesbian sexuality to depravity.

It is clear that while the vampires, who are always aristocratic ladies with long family bloodlines, seduce and initiate relationships with other aristocratic ladies, they demonstrate a clear class bias in their seemingly random attacks on and murders of peasants, servant girls, and other lower-class women. These mere peasant girls are dispensable in the film's development, but the violent attacks on them are not: they serve to unite the titillation and the threat of gratuitous violence.

In a scene from another Hammer film, *Twins of Evil,* one of the two female twins has just become a vampire. As she begins to attack a local peasant girl (chained to the wall), there is a brief, unspoken, erotic exchange between the two women: the victim momentarily responds to the vampire's advances, and they seem about to kiss, when the vampire attacks. We hear a scream—and the shot dissolves into a close-up on the face of a male vampire, previously in the corner of the frame voyeuristically watching the encounter, now laughing wickedly. The lesbian sexual overtones of the violence are pronounced, monitored by the male gaze from the edge of the frame, and confirmed by the laughter that expresses his pleasure in looking. Lesbian scenes from the third film in the Hammer trilogy, *Lust for a Vampire,* are also consistently framed in relationship to an on-screen male voyeur: one man watches as two naked women swim and kiss in the moonlight; another listens; calls out and pounds on the door behind which two women make vampiric love.

*Blood and Roses,* directed by Roger Vadim in 1960, is a film which, unlike the later Hammer Films productions, avoids the excessive blood and graphic sexual images associated with the genre. Instead, it is more closely related to the European art-cinema tradition with its emphasis on lush, provocative, visual imagery over a straightforward, coherent narrative. In one beautiful scene, the vampire Carmilla (Annette Vadim) attacks Liza, a servant girl. Here, it is ambiguous whether the vampire is pursuing sex or violence; the film's visual style barely distinguishes between them. The music, Cinemascope pastoral imagery, and moving camera (a slow tracking shot of the two women running through the landscape) contribute to what seems to be, at first, a romantic seduction scene that eventually turns on itself and becomes violent. We don't see the violence, but we see Liza's expression of fear, hear her scream at the end of the scene, and subsequently learn that she is dead. Even in *Blood and Roses,* which avoids the typical exploitation approach, sexuality and violence are visually coupled, as complementary qualities intrinsic to a lesbian relationship.

Another cultural myth to which the lesbian vampire film

subscribes maintains that lesbians are narcissistic. This is most blatant in the use of twins in *Twins of Evil* and in the scene from *The Vampire Lovers* that immediately follows the bedroom scene described earlier. After Carmilla and Emma emerge from the bedroom, they walk down the stairs together, with their hair, dress, and expressions identical. Whereas previously the difference between them was emphasized (Carmilla older, stronger, aggressive, more sophisticated; Emma younger, weaker, passive, more naïve), following the seduction scene they have become narcissistically matched.

Another, related cultural myth asserts that lesbian sexuality is infantile: in the *Twins of Evil* scene described above, the vampire goes not for the throat, but in a gesture that makes reference to infantile obsession, the victim's breast. There are similar scenes in all of the Hammer Films productions, in which breast imagery dominates the screen and is given anxious attention through accentuating clothes and symbolic displacement. Both solid and fluid, and representing mother and lover, breasts—like the vampire's mouth—symbolically embrace contradictions. In *Twins of Evil,* the breast imagery creates a kind of visual spectacle, to deflect the spectator's attention away from the contradictions generated by the film—the contradictions of constructing an image of active and dangerous female desire which is circumscribed and defined by male spectatorial pleasure. At the same time, the breast fetishism helps reduce lesbian desire to an infantile, pre-Oedipal phase of development.

One way the narrative structure enforces these cultural myths is by closing down the range of possible alternative interpretations that spectators can read from the film. In

*The Vampire Lovers,* this is done in part by framing the entire plot of the film from the perspective of a male narrator, a famous vampire hunter, who appears on-screen only in the opening and closing sequences and who gives a voice-over narration leading the audience into the film's events. It is interesting that, with this one exception of the male narrator, the entire plot of *The Vampire Lovers* otherwise follows very closely the plot of the Victorian novel *Carmilla.* Screenwriter Tudor Gates recalls that Hammer Studios was able to sell the idea of *The Vampire Lovers* on the basis of a lurid poster and a three-page outline, and the outline described this opening scene of the vampire hunter.[13] The male narrator is therefore the screenwriter's pure fabrication, created for the purpose of raising financing, but having the additional benefit of enabling male viewers to be sexually aroused by the film with the assurance that the controlling voice of the narrative is male. After his introduction, the film retreats immediately to a detached, impersonal form of address that masks this male subjectivity behind a seemingly objective "narrative truth."

An important characteristic of the lesbian vampire is that she relies far more on her sexual powers than on her supernatural powers—in fact, her sexual powers are usually equated with supernatural powers. In the early days of the cinema, the word "vampire" had a meaning similar to "vamp": a beautiful woman whose sexual desire, if fulfilled, would drain the lifeblood of man. This mortal vampire was an extremely popular character in early films. The earliest such film, *The Vampire,* was made in 1910. It was reviewed that year in the *New York Dramatic Mirror* as being about "a beautiful woman who delighted in ruining men." Between 1914 and 1916, the classic "vampire" was played by Theda

Bara in such films as *A Fool There Was* (1914) and *Sin*
(1915). Theda Bara's real name was Theodosia Goodman
and she was the daughter of a Jewish garment worker;
voluptuous and dark, her image was linked to evil sexuality, helping to define and keep "pure" the more common
blonde virgin image. But if men projected dangerous sexuality on Theda Bara, female spectators could find in her
role the pleasure of revenge. Bara herself once said, "Women
were my greatest fans because they see in my [role as] vampire the impersonal vengeance of all their unavenged
wrongs.... I have the face of a vampire, perhaps, but the
heart of a feministe."[14] In the first decade of the cinema
there were at least forty films about this mortal female
vampire, whom men could find sexually enticing while
women could fantasize female empowerment.

In the most recent lesbian vampire film, *The Hunger*
(1980), the vampire's power is still purely sexual, even
though now she is also endowed with supernatural qualities.
In a scene famous to lesbian audiences, the sophisticated,
aristocratic Catherine Deneuve seduces the more butch
Susan Sarandon, and Susan Sarandon is so enticed by the
sexual rather than the supernatural that they are already
undressed and well under way before we are reminded,
through images of a blood exchange, that one of the women
is a vampire.

As a measure of this scene's importance to lesbian spectators, a debate has been generated within lesbian circles
as to the "authenticity" of the sex between Deneuve and
Sarandon. Some lesbians claim that Deneuve is not actually
in the scene, but rather a body double is used in her place,
a rumor which is often told with considerable disappoint-
ment. However, the truth of the rumor (a body double *is*

intercut with shots of Deneuve) seems less important than its existence in the first place, which suggests that lesbians have spent a lot of time scrutinizing this scene on their home VCRs, giving the vampire relationship a kind of legitimacy as a viable representation of lesbianism, and acknowledging its erotic potential for women.[15]

The vampire character in *The Hunger* is not based on Carmilla, but on a second source: the legend of Countess Elisabeth Báthory of Transylvania, who lived in the seventeenth century. From most accounts, she was a sexual sadist who tortured and murdered her female servants and later progressed to local noblewomen before she was caught and brought to trial. This blight on the Hungarian aristocratic landscape was immediately hushed up by church and state, and the incriminating trial testimony was considered so shocking that it was suppressed for over a hundred years.[16]

In the absence of historical fact, the Hungarian imagination worked overtime to fill the void. The Báthory legend spread like wildfire through villages and towns across Eastern Europe throughout the seventeenth, eighteenth, and nineteenth centuries. One of the most popular myths about her is that she murdered young virgins because she believed that bathing in their blood would restore her youth.

Although this myth provides the plot of the Hammer film *Countess Dracula* (Peter Sasdy, 1971), in *The Hunger* the vampire is only indirectly based on the Elisabeth Báthory legend, modernizing the icon of the irresistible aristocratic woman and her ability to keep her youth at her victims' expense. But another lesbian vampire film, *Daughters of Darkness,* relies more closely on the Báthory story.

*Daughters of Darkness* (Harry Kumel, Belgium, 1970)

has enjoyed something of a cult following, not only because it stars Delphine Seyrig, but also because, in many ways, it tends deliberately to subvert the lesbian vampire genre. For example, instead of the male voyeur watching the lesbians make love, the lesbian vampire and her lover stand outside the window and watch the heterosexual couple. Also, the vampire, Elisabeth Báthory, is the most likable character in the film. According to the standard bisexual-triangle formula discussed earlier, she would represent a threat or obstacle to the heterosexual norm that the narrative of most lesbian vampire films seeks to overcome. But here, the heterosexual norm turns out to be frighteningly abnormal and nightmarish (the man who is competing against the vampire turns out to be a closet homosexual and sadistic toward women), and the lifestyle of the lesbian vampire seems like a welcome alternative. In one scene, the vampire uses a feminist critique of male behavior toward women and of heterosexuality in general, rather than any supernatural power she has, to lure her "victim" away from the man. Elisabeth Báthory (Delphine Seyrig) mocks Valerie's (Andrea Rau's) allegiance to her husband and her claim that "Stefan loves me, whatever you think," by answering, "That's why he wants to make of you what every man wants of every woman. A slave, a thing, an object for pleasure."

The degree of narrative closure largely influences what meanings the lesbian vampire films can generate, and the extent to which lesbians can find alternative or oppositional meanings. In the conclusion of a typical bisexual-triangle film—*Personal Best, The Bostonians*—given an even fight between a heterosexual man and a lesbian, the man will win every time, thereby restoring the "natural order." Heterosexuality triumphs over homosexuality, and man triumphs over woman. The typical lesbian vampire film concludes by following this same scenario, but the man must invariably kill the lesbian character in order to destroy the threat she represents. Although lesbian characters are frequently killed off in any film's conclusion *(The Fox, The Children's Hour),* mainstream Hollywood films do not usually allow their lesbian characters to act on their sexual desire. The horror film, in contrast, has an added punishment to mete out: the lesbian vampire is killed because of her active sexuality as well as her lesbianism. Seemingly sexually "liberated" from the restraints of Hollywood, the lesbian vampire film appears to allow for women's desire but always exacts its punishment. The theorist Raymond Bellour has written:

> The masculine subject can accept the image of woman's pleasure only on the condition that, having constructed it, he may inscribe himself within it, and thus reappropriate it even at the cost of its (or her) destruction.[17]

Linda Williams has pushed this observation further, and found that "the titillating attention given to the expression of women's desire is directly proportional to the violence perpetrated [within the film] against women."[18]

The lesbian vampire must lose to the mortal man in the battle for possession of the mortal woman. In such a battle scene from *The Vampire Lovers,* perfect symmetry is achieved: the scene opens with Carmilla carrying Emma down the stairs, and ends with Karl, the male victor, carrying Emma back up the stairs. Carmilla's attempt to take Emma away with her is interrupted; the scene is intercut with Karl racing up on his white horse. He enters the house, the struggle takes place, and with the help of the cross (a vampire repellent), good triumphs over evil. Emma, like the spoils of war, has changed hands, and the audience supposedly sighs with relief.

The typical lesbian vampire film, belonging within the horror/exploitation genre, is an articulation of men's subconscious fear of and hostility toward women's sexuality. The lesbian vampire seduction embodies myths common not only to vampirism but to women's sexuality as it traditionally has been defined in the cinema, and links the fear of vampirism with the male fear of women. The vampire's thirst for blood and the association of blood with menstruation makes mocking reference to female life-giving capacities, inverting them into life-taking ones. The lesbian vampire film uses lesbianism as titillation that is at once provocative and conquerable, and equates lesbian sexual powers with unnatural powers. It appeals to deep, dark fears of the insatiable female, the consuming mother, the devouring mother, woman as monster, the "vagina dentata." To the extent that seduction rather than violent coercion implies some degree of complicity, it depicts a consensual relationship between two women as inherently pathological, with the self-preservation of the one appealing to the self-destructiveness of the other. One woman's survival is always at the other's expense.

If the lesbian vampire dramatizes men's fears, anxieties, and hatred of women, is it possible for lesbians to derive pleasure from such films? The lesbian vampire is the most powerful representation of lesbianism to be found on the commercial movie screen; and rather than abandon her for what she signifies, it may be possible to extricate her from her original function, and reappropriate her power.

James Donald has argued that the vampire film does "present the Other as a threat..." but it is not limited to this function. He writes that vampire films "are not just ideological mechanisms for domesticating terror and repression in popular culture...[but are] also symptoms of the instability of culture, the impossibility of its closure or perfection." [19] In the lesbian vampire films that fall outside of the low-budget horror/exploitation genre, this impossibility of cultural closure is paralleled precisely by an impossibility of narrative closure, which in turn lends itself to alternative viewing strategies by lesbian spectators. Drawing heavily on European art-cinema conventions, the films *Blood and Roses, The Hunger,* and *Daughters of Darkness* use higher production budgets, well-known actors and directors, and do not rely on violence and nudity to hold the viewer. But it is not their art-film status so much as their more ambiguous endings (which is, after all, an art-cinema characteristic) which allow for a wider range of readings. In these conclusions, the vampire is still physically destroyed, but the woman whom she seduced becomes a vampire herself through the transmigration of the vampire's soul. And as the lesbian vampire lives on in a new body, the cycle that is set in motion by her first appearance continues beyond the film's ending. Because of this, these films can be seen as departures from the genre, even as they draw heavily from it. Bonnie Zimmerman has suggested that *Daughters of Darkness* is open to lesbian reinterpretation because of the romantic, trans-historical appeal of the film's ending, in which the vampire's spirit "occupies a new body once it is deprived of the old, suggesting that lesbianism is eternal, passing effortlessly from one woman to another."[20]

Lesbians can also find erotic elements in scenes which do

not feature direct displays of sexuality. This is certainly true of *Dracula's Daughter,* and perhaps *Blood and Roses* as well. In *Dracula's Daughter,* produced in 1936, the spectator's sympathy is with the vampire (Gloria Holden). With the advent of psychology as a more widely accepted field of science, lesbianism and vampirism are presented as uncontrollable afflictions for which the tormented lesbian vampire herself seeks professional help. The countess tries, but fails, to escape her family heritage of vampirism; she seduces young women before being destroyed by the doctor who failed to cure her. Gloria Holden is beautiful, and the film is elegantly stylized in black-and-white, elements which help make the film pleasurable for contemporary (if not also historical) lesbian audiences. In *Blood and Roses* (1960), external events such as a masquerade ball and a fireworks display are used to suggest Carmilla's inner turmoil; such events are also symbols for the film's repressed lesbianism, which emerges in only a few, very restrained scenes. There may be pleasure for lesbian viewers in the discovery of these subtextual lesbian scenes, and in reading them as lesbian.

While *The Vampire Lover* uses the male vampire hunter as a stand-in for the perspective of the male spectator, *Blood and Roses* uses a similar voice-over narration device; but here it is the voice of Carmilla herself, telling her own story. This shift in the position of the narrator contributes to lesbian spectators' pleasure in the vampire's seductions; it is as though she has made a pact with the lesbian viewer, which turns her into an accomplice.

Lesbian vampire films can further encourage a unique reception by lesbian spectators because of the powerful erotic connotations of the vampire relationship and its expression of a secret and forbidden sexuality. But, more commonly, certain problems of representation and spectatorship work against such a reception. The typical vampire and her victim are both visually coded as heterosexual and feminine, even though the narrative sets them up to be lovers. They lack the lesbian verisimilitude that would enable them to "pass" as lesbians; they flirt with men and dress (and undress) to appeal to male desire. If they do not offer the same image of erotic fascination for women that they are intended to provide for heterosexual men, neither do they pose the same threat for lesbian viewers as they do for men. As a result, the lesbian spectator's relationship to the vampire takes a different form: neither sexually desirable nor sexually threatening, the lesbian vampire is appealing only for the power she wields. Instead of feeling endangered, lesbians can derive vicarious enjoyment from the vampire's dangerous powers. But, due to her unique position, the lesbian spectator doesn't develop a fear of the vampire. And, of course, as a horror film, it then falls flat. Without the element of danger, the film becomes a burlesque, to be appreciated primarily as camp.

Although usually considered to be the province of gay male culture, camp is a frequent component of lesbian spectatorship as well, arising from the relationship between theatrical and melodramatic qualities in the cinema on the one hand, and those perceptions of the world which are informed by one's gayness, on the other. Critic Jack Babuscio has identified four features basic to the definition of camp: irony, aestheticism, theatricality, and humor. His definition is a useful starting point for understanding the subversive strategies of camp for lesbian spectators. Certainly there is irony in the lesbian vampire film. The lesbian vampire is incongruous socially; she is not what she seems to be, and her difference is not detected by those around her despite some obvious signs. This incongruity can be especially appreciated by lesbians who often find themselves in a similar social situation.

Furthermore, camp identifies itself through artifice and aestheticism, rejecting and opposing puritan morality.[21] Since lesbian spectators can dismiss the puritan morality represented by the vampire hunters (good Christian men), they are freer to enjoy the film's exaggerated, predictable imagery and obvious theatricality, the vampire's "masking of 'abnormality' behind a facade of 'normality.'"[22]

Finally, camp relies on humor. Babuscio writes: "Camp can...be a means of undercutting rage by its derision of concentrated bitterness. Its vision of the world is comic."[23] Camp humor is a way of exposing and disempowering those cultural myths and representations which would otherwise be unrelentingly oppressive, especially to women and gay people. Susan Sontag calls camp "a solvent of morality [which] neutralizes moral indignation."[24] An example of lesbian spectators' use of camp to displace immobilizing rage and indignation can be found in relation to yet another horror film whose victims are female. At a gay-liberation film series in the early 1970s in New York, during a screening of *Invasion of the Body Snatchers,* a lesbian yelled out from the back of the audience, "Save me a breast!"[25]

The dominant cinema demands that men do the looking and that women are looked at. The lesbian vampire breaks through this cinematic relationship and actively looks. She remains the object of male desire but also becomes the agent for female desire—dangerous, excessive, lesbian desire. This contradiction begs the question: Can cultural myths about the "dark side" of women's sexuality be reworked into a framework which is empowering rather than victimizing? Recent lesbian vampire films by independent filmmakers—such as Bruna Fionda, Polly Gladwin, and Isiling Mack-Nataf's *Mark of Lilith* (Great Britain, 1986) and Amy Goldstein's highly stylized *Because the Dawn* (United States, 1988)—begin to explore this possibility. The former raises the question of where such a process of reappropriation might lead, while the latter reverses the power relation so that it is the vampire who is desired—the mortal woman stalks the streets at night in search of her. But even if such a complete "revamping" of the genre is ultimately not possible, a complete reading provides a powerful antidote. Camp creates the space for an identification with the vampire's secret, forbidden sexuality which doesn't also demand participation in one's own victimization as a requisite for cinematic pleasure.

## Notes

1. Bertha Harris, "What is a Lesbian?" *Sinister Wisdom*, 3 (1977).
2. Richard Dyer, "It's In Their Kiss: Vampirism as Homosexuality, Homosexuality as Vampirism," unpublished paper, 5.
3. Susan Sontag, "Persona," *Sight and Sound*, 36.4 (Autumn 1967) pp. 186, 191.
4. Lillian Faderman, *Surpassing the Love of Men* (New York: William Morrow and Co., 1981) pp. 341-6.
5. Gene Damon, *The Ladder* (February/March 1971) p. 36; (June/July 1971) pp. 47-8.
6. Conversation with Tudor Gates, screenwriter of the Hammer lesbian vampire trilogy, on January 16, 1992, London.
7. Bonnie Zimmerman, "Daughters of Darkness: Lesbian Vampires," *Jump Cut*, 24/25 (Fall 1980) p.23.
8. James Donald, "The Fantastic, the Sublime, and the Popular, or What's At Stake in Vampire Films?," *Fantasy and the Cinema,* ed. James Donald (London: British Film Institute, 1989) p. 237.
9. Christopher Craft, "Kiss Me with Those Ruby Lips: Gender and Inversion in Bram Stoker's *Dracula*," *Representations*, 8 (Fall 1984) p. 109.
10. This fascination with the genitals of female "inverts" in the turn of the century is discussed in George Chauncey, Jr., "From Sexual Inversion to Homosexuality: Medicine and the Changing Conceptualization of Female Deviance," *Salmagundi*, 58-59 (1982), pp. 114-46.
11. Craft, "Kiss Me," p. 109.
12. Linda Williams, "When the Woman Looks," *Revision: Feminist Essays in Film Analysis*, ed. Mary Ann Doane, Patricia Mellencamp and Linda Williams (Washington, D.C.: American Film Institute, 1984) p. 87.
13. Conversation with Tudor Gates, screenwriter, on January 16, 1992, London.

14. Theda Bara, interviewed in *Theatre Magazine* (June 1917) p. 246, cited in Lary May, *Screening Out the Past: The Birth of Mass Culture and the Motion Picture Industry* (New York: Oxford University Press, 1980).

15. This "body double" rumor was first brought to my attention by the writer Michelle Cliff, in conversation in July 1991.

16. The life and legends of Elisabeth Báthory are discussed in Raymond T. McNally, *Dracula Was a Woman* (New York: McGraw Hill, 1983) and David Pirie, *The Vampire Cinema* (Quanto, 1977).

17. Raymond Bellour, "psychosis, neurosis, perversion," *Camera Obscura*, 3/4 (1979) p. 121.

18. Williams, "When the Woman Looks," p. 97.

19. Donald, "The Fantastic, Sublime, and the Popular," p. 247.

20. Zimmerman, "Daughters of Darkness," p. 24.

21. Sontag, "Notes on Camp."

22. Babuscio, "Camp and the Gay Sensibility," p. 43.

23. Ibid. p. 48.

24. Sontag, "Notes on Camp," p. 275.

25. At the early 1970s Film Series organized by Vito Russo at the Gay Liberation "Firehouse" in New York City, recounted by Arnie Kantrowitz on the occasion of Vito Russo's memorial service, November 1990.

JENNI OLSON
# Butch Icons of the Silver Screen

When I was little, I could recognize myself in the faces and screen characters of Tatum O'Neal, Jodie Foster, and Kristy McNichol. These little tomboys empowered me to think of myself as a hero. They were strong and smart like the movie cowboys and gangsters I emulated. They were "different" and the difference was celebrated on-screen as good old-fashioned individuality.

On screen, tomboys were socially acceptable. As a young butch dyke coming out in 1986, I looked for their grown-up counterparts. I couldn't find anything. My trio of tomboy heroes hadn't turned out like I had. Instead, I turned to Marlon Brando and James Dean as my role models of butch-ness.

Then, when I was a twenty-three-year-old film studies major at the University of Minnesota, Vito Russo's book *The Celluloid Closet* opened the door to a vast world of lesbian and gay film images—a new landscape of culture, heroes, and recognition. I don't remember how I got my hands on it, but I do remember that I couldn't put it down.

I wanted to see the films Vito wrote about. Not just on video in the privacy of my own home, but with an audience full of people who wanted to see them as badly as I did. With lists of film titles in my head, I approached the student film committee with my proposal for "Lavender Images: A Lesbian and Gay Film Retrospective." Their unenthusiastic approval left me alone and uncertain in front of a shelf full of 16mm distribution catalogs. Finding the source for *The Killing of Sister George* after hours of searching, I began my career as a film programmer. I also began my own informal inventory (and source list) of butch women in film.

The films included here are all feature-length motion pictures, mostly Hollywood productions, some independently produced. Most of these films are available for rental on video. A brief list of mail-order distributors specializing in lesbian and gay films on video is included along with listings of nontheatrical distributors for specific titles (in case you want to present your own Butch Film Festival). There are many interesting works dealing with gender issues and butchness being produced in short-format film and video, and a brief listing of some of these films is also included.

### Tomboy

•Robin Johnson. *Times Square;* Allan Moyle, USA (1980). Robin Johnson's cocky, streetwise Nicky is one of the sweetest dyke portrayals ever. She's tough and romantic, shy and insecure; she's a hero, she's a gravel-voiced, tough-talking, rock-'n'-roll icon. She does the butch/femme thing with Pammy (Trini Alvarado) as they play off each other's strengths and insecurities like the classic lesbian couple. "I'm brave, but you're pretty. I'm a fuckin' freak of nature," she tells Pammy. While there's no explicit lesbian content in the film, the original script had several scenes and plot elements that developed the sexual butch/femme tension between Nicky and Pammy, including: their first meeting in the hospital in which they have to undress in front of each other; two scenes where they take off their shirts and play together in their underwear in the river; a wrestling scene; the first night that they sleep (sleep, not fuck) together; and a scene where Pammy dances topless at the Cleo Club while Nicky watches. Despite all this missing content, there's tons of erotic tension between the girls. Most importantly, they love each other, and they're not interested in boys.

Also see:

•Little Jodie Foster in everything she was in before she grew up and her voice changed—especially Gary Nelson's *Freaky Friday,* USA (1976) and Nicolas Gessner's *The Little Girl Who Lives Down the Lane,* USA (1976).

•Little Tatum O'Neal in Peter Bogdanovich's *Paper Moon,* USA (1973), Michael Ritchie's *Bad News Bears,* USA (1976), and Ronald F. Maxwell's *Little Darlings,* USA (1980). She's not actually all that butch in *Little Darlings,* but she's very cute, and it's such a great movie. She and Kristy McNichol and the other girls are all so in love with each other that you can read it as an allegory of closeted lesbian adolescence. Kristy McNichol, of course, is the butch one. As Kristy and Tatum race to lose their virginity, Kristy's the one who sleeps with a boy—and you know it's really to prove that she's not a dyke. But you know that she *is* a dyke—which makes it a really moving film. I saw this in a theater when I was seventeen, and I identified on an intensely uncomfortable level with Kristy McNichol. It was a very strange experience to see my awkward tomboy self in a Hollywood movie. And Kristy probably wasn't acting; she was just being herself as the uncomfortable-in-her-body, Marlboro-smoking, teenage butch with the jean jacket and seventies adolescent girl bad haircut.

•Mary Stuart Masterson in Howard Deutsch's *Some Kind of Wonderful,* USA (1987). She gets dirty, she plays drums, she pretends she's interested in Eric Stultz, but she doesn't actually do anything about it. There's all kinds of coded dialogue about her being "different" from other girls. And she's totally cute. Way better than her Annie Hall–butch Idgy in *Fried Green Tomatoes.*

•Mercedes McCambridge (in a small, uncredited part) as the dykey Chicana juvenile delinquent in Orson Welles's *Touch of Evil,* USA (1958). When the boys ask the girls to leave the room as they prepare to gang-rape Janet Leigh, McCambridge insists, "I wanna watch."

•Julie Harris as Frankie in Fred Zinneman's *Member of the Wedding,* USA (1953).

### FTM (Women as Men/Girls as Boys)

•Tomoko Otakra, Rie Mizuhara, Miyuki Nakano, and Eri Miyagima. *Summer Vacation: 1999;* Shusuke Kaneko, Japan (1988). *Summer Vacation* looks at the shifting attractions between four boys at an isolated country school. Vivid character development, clever narrative structure, and a striking visual atmosphere come together in this beautiful cinematic fantasy. In a brilliant genderbending casting twist, director Kaneko cast girls in the male roles, later dubbing in their voices with those of four male actors. While most Western audiences are familiar with the *Noh / Kabuki* tradition of Japanese theater in which female roles are played by men, *Summer Vacation* draws on the less-known *Taburazuka* tradition, in which male roles are played by women.

• Pamela Segall. *Something Special;* Paul Schneider, USA (1985). In this obscure teen transgender comedy, Milly Niceman wishes she were a boy and then wakes in the middle of the night to discover she's magically grown "a guy's thing down there." Her family and friends make the adjustment to her new male self, Willy, and the film plays extensively on all of the homo- and lesbo-erotic potentials available. She goes back to being a girl at the end (so she can be with a boy), but she's still a butch girl even if she is straight.

• Anne Carlisle. *Liquid Sky;* Slava Tsukerman, USA (1983). Anne Carlisle's performance as queer twin brother and sister is one of the sexiest examples of androgyny ever filmed. As original as they come, this sci-fi sex-and-drug story is raw, funny, and strangely moving. (I fell in love with Anne Carlisle after seeing this film and ran to the video store to find anything else she was in; the only thing I could find was a really boring drama in which she looks and acts completely normal. Resist the temptation to rent it— I can't even remember its name—just watch *Liquid Sky* again.)

• Marta Keler. *Virgina;* Srdjan Karanovic, Yugoslavia/ France (1991). *Virgina* offers a remarkable look at the workings of misogyny, gender, and sex roles in nineteenth-century Serbia. The film's title is taken from the Serbian term used in describe a girl raised as a boy. This practice seems to have been not entirely uncommon; according to superstition, lack of a son would bring about the family's demise. Born as the fourth daughter of a poor Serbian family, "Stephen" narrowly escapes being shot at birth by her father. Raised as a boy, Stephen sees her mother and sisters treated abusively by her father. Her empathy for them as a woman is countered by her family's insistence that she indulge her own male privilege. Her mother consoles her, "Better a rooster for a day than a hen for life. Everything is made for men." Growing up to be a handsome young boy, Stephen finds a boyfriend and a girlfriend, and a good deal of erotic tension with both. A tragedy provokes Stephen's eventual rebellion against her father, and in a surprising revelation, Stephen's masquerade is shown to be a common thread in the fabric of this androcentric Serbian culture. The film was completed during the outbreak of the civil war in June 1991.

Also see:

• Eva Mattes. *A Man Like Eva,* Radu Gabrea, Germany (1983). Eva Mattes stars as Rainer Werner Fassbinder in this rather slow, fictionalized portrayal of the late, great, gay director.

## FTMTF (Women as Men Who Become Women)

• Vanessa Redgrave. *Second Serve;* Anthony Page, USA (1986). Redgrave is so convincing as a man in the first part of this made-for-television bio-pic of tennis coach Renée Richards that it's hard to believe she's a woman in the second part.

Also see:

• Anne Heywood as Roy/Wendy in John Dexter's *I Want*

*What I Want,* USA (1972). Heywood (*The Fox*) is totally weird (not really butch, but very queer) in this bizarre sex-change melodrama. The film ultimately comes across as a plea for transsexual understanding as Roy becomes Wendy and falls in love with a man. A camp gem with much unintentional humor. Watch for the period styles in home furnishings, hair, clothing, and especially makeup.

• Micheline Carvel in *Adam Is Eve,* France (1953).

### Gender Dysphoria

• Ana Beatriz Nogueira. *Vera;* Sergio Toledo, Brazil (1986). Presenting the story of a young woman who believes that she is a man, *Vera* deals with issues of masculine/butch identification and internalized misogyny and portrays the dysfunctional effects of rigid gender-role stratification. Vera does not identify herself as a lesbian (she believes she's a man in a woman's body). Vera grows up in an orphanage then, on being released when she turns eighteen, takes a job at a research center where she meets Clara, with whom she falls in love. Vera's insistence that she is a man becomes problematic when, in a painfully intimate love scene, she refuses to remove her undershirt. The relationship between Clara and Vera is seriously jeopardized as they both struggle with Vera's gender dysphoria. Two notes about the film: the film employs an unusually fluid, and at times hard-to-follow, flashback structure to show parts of Vera's life in the orphanage. An ambiguous ending (open to two very different interpretations) makes the film extremely disturbing.

Also see:

• Mink Stole in John Waters's *Desperate Living,* USA (1977). When her girlfriend says she doesn't like her sex change, she cuts off her cock with a scissors and throws it out the door.

## General Genderfuck

•Shelley Mars. *The Virgin Machine;* Monika Treut, West Germany (1988). Shelley Mars does double-duty drag: as Ramona the sex therapist, she poses in the stylized lesbian fuck scene with Ira Blum; and as Martin the sleazy male chauvinist pig, she performs her famous Burlezk drag/strip routine. He strips down to his shirttails and boxer shorts, jacks off a beer bottle, and cums foam all over the stage.

•Ellen Barkin. *Switch;* Blake Edwards, USA (1992). A truly weird rendering of what could have been a predictable retread. Barkin as Amanda/Steve plays up the slapstick and sexism of masculinity and goes a bit over the top on the artifice of femininity. His/her budding feminist consciousness provides plenty of cathartic moments (a là *Thelma and Louise*), and there's homo-lesbo-eroticism everywhere. The ad campaign for *Switch* posed the genderfuck question of the year: "Will being a woman make him a better man?" There *was* an extensive girl/girl love scene between Ellen Barkin and Lorraine Bracco; unfortunately the scene was cut after test audiences responded negatively to it at prescreenings of the film. In a cover story interview, "The Sexiest Man Alive," in *Entertainment Weekly,* Barkin said of the excised love scene: "There was no nudity or anything, but it was a lot heavier than what's in the film now. [Director] Blake [Edwards] didn't want to cut it. And to me it really elevated the film. But the audiences weren't ready for that. I felt that [Blake and the studio] should have just shoved it down their throats. It would have been a great thing for gay women." As Barkin describes the final version of the scene, it sounds a bit too much like what Stephen Spielberg did to the love scene between Celie and Shug in his "version" of *The Color Purple.* Barkin says, "Lorraine and I came up with this idea that my character would get the giggles and out of nerves have uncontrollable fits of laughter while Lorraine was very seriously trying to make love to her." Alas, another Hollywood lesbian love scene goes down (as it were) in history, right alongside the tickling scene in *Personal Best.* Who says lesbians don't have a sense of humor? Looking at Hollywood, it seems that's *all* we have. We certainly don't have sex.

•Carole Landis. *Turnabout;* Hal Roach, USA (1940). Husband and wife change bodies halfway through this screwball comedy. The comic talents of Carole Landis bring a measure of intelligence and hilarity to a fairly lightweight script. She dresses up in big man clothes and mimics male body language, speech, and gesture.

•Veronica Lake. *Sullivan's Travels;* Preston Sturges, USA (1941). The plot makes no use at all of Veronica Lake's boy-drag as she dresses up to go slumming with Joel McCrea. (As they walk through a shantytown holding hands, director Sturges seems oblivious to any notion of homo-eroticism.) The film's feel-good populism (a là Frank Capra) focuses on Joel McCrea as Everyman, and Lake is, of course, merely a woman. She steals the film from McCrea when she's on-screen and (along with Bacall and Dietrich) has one of the sexiest deep voices ever heard—they call it "sultry" when femmes talk that way.

## Passing

• Katharine Hepburn. *Sylvia Scarlett;* George Cukor, USA (1936). Hepburn previously did a bit of cross-dressing in Dorothy Arzner's 1933 woman-aviator melodrama, *Christopher Strong.* Here she goes all out as Sylvester Scarlett, boy thief and traveling musician. It's a crazy plot that veers bizarrely from comedy to tragedy. As with Garbo's *Queen Christina,* the latter half of the film is disappointing. But Hepburn's a bundle of boy energy, looks like a young David Bowie, and even has a girl kiss her on the lips.

• Greta Garbo. *Queen Christina;* Rouben Mamoulian, USA (1933). The one-and-only Garbo gives the drag performance of her career as the titular seventeenth-century queen. Swaggering about castle and countryside in male attire, the Swedish queen is as butch as they come, and then some. Although the real-life queen was a lesbian, the film has her falling in love with John Gilbert. Just underneath the heterosexual act, however, is a clear queer appeal, and it's easy to imagine the queen as a dyke. Christina's apparent love interest through the first half of the film is the Countess Ebba Sparre (Elizabeth Young), and an early scene in the film features a very nice butch/femme sort of kiss between the two.

When Christina meets Antonio (John Gilbert) in a country inn (where she is traveling in male disguise), they end up having to share a room together. In a very provocative sequence of misgendered identities, the queen is propositioned by a barmaid. She reveals to Antonio that she is a woman, and, on waking in bed together the following morning, the couple is seen by a servant who raises his eyebrows at the two "men."

When pressed by her valet to marry ("But Your Majesty, you cannot die an old maid"), the queen replies, "I have no intention to... I shall die a bachelor."

Indeed, Garbo herself died a bachelor, and at this point her own lesbianism is common knowledge. The behind-the-scenes history of this film (according to Mercedes D'Acosta's autobiography) is that Garbo and D'Acosta, who had been lovers, developed the film together. Later D'Acosta was fired as screenwriter from the project because she was making it too clear that the queen was a lesbian. This seems to come through quite clearly in the beginning of the film, and changes somewhat strangely when the queen has a fight with the countess somewhere in the second reel. Thereafter, the queen toys with the affections of a court ambassador (who obviously does not interest her) until she meets Antonio. When she gives up her throne to be with Antonio (in real life she gave it up to be with Ebba Sparre), the film makes its ultimate break with reality.

In *The Celluloid Closet,* Vito Russo cites the following excerpt from a 1933 *New York Herald-Tribune* book review which makes reference to the anticipated release of the film: "The one persistent love of Christina's life was for the Countess Ebba Sparre, a beautiful Swedish noblewoman who lost most of her interest in Christina when Christina ceased to rule Sweden...the evidence is overwhelming, but will Miss Garbo play such a Christina?" Unfortunately no. Small consolation—Antonio dies and Christina goes off alone in the end.

Also see:

•Julie Andrews in Blake Edwards's *Victor/Victoria,* USA (1982). Remember *The Sound of Music?* Julie Andrews doesn't really seem very convincing as a man, does she?

•Barbra Streisand in her own *Yentl,* USA (1983). Another Barbra Streisand movie I didn't see.

•Molly Picon in Joseph Green's *Yiddle with His Fiddle,* Poland (1937). A movie Barbra Streisand saw before she made *Yentl.*

•Anne Bancroft. *Seven Women;* John Ford, USA (1966). Bancroft struts her stuff as the chain-smoking, cowboy-cross-dressing Dr. Cartwright. She's tough, bold, intelligent, and doesn't take shit from anyone (until the end, when she is forced—albeit heroically—into a submissive role). The film also features Margaret Leighton as Agatha Andrews, the repressed lesbian spinster with the hots for Sue Lyon. Set in 1935 China, in an all-women mission, *Seven Women* is remarkable for offering an intense psychological study of its female characters. Unfortunately, the portrayal of the film's Mongolian robbers is not so enlightened, falling into the usual Hollywood racist stereotypes in the last half of the picture.

•Joan Crawford and Mercedes McCambridge. *Johnny Guitar;* Nicholas Ray, USA (1954). More cowboy drag, and good feudin' between Joan and Mercedes.

Also see:

•Betty Hutton in 501s and facial hair in the "Oh Them Dudes" production number in *Let's Dance,* USA (1950); Beverly Garland in Roger Corman's *Gunslinger,* USA (1956); Jane Russell in *Montana Belle,* USA (1952); Doris Day in *Calamity Jane,* USA (1953); Louise Dresser in *Caught,* USA (1931): Martha Sleeper in *West of the Pecos,* USA (1934); Barbara Hale in *West of the Pecos,* USA (1945); and Dorothy Gish in *Nugget Nell,* USA (1919).

Last but not least, check out Suzi Quatro as Leather Tuscadero in TV's "Happy Days."

## Law Enforcement

• Jodie Foster. *Silence of the Lambs;* Jonathan Demme, USA (1991). She has the sexiest butch hands.

• Jamie Lee Curtis. *Blue Steel;* Kathryn Bigelow, USA (1990). A stupid ending (her sleeping with the big he-man cop), but who can resist a girl with a gun?

Also see:

• Hope Emerson in her Academy Award-nominated portrayal of the sadistic prison matron Evelyn Harper in John Cromwell's *Caged,* USA (1950). Also Eleanor Parker in the last half of the film (after she gets her head shaved).

## Strong Female Characters Who Look Really Butch When They're All Sweaty and Dirty

• Sigourney Weaver and Jenette Goldstein. *Aliens;* Ridley Scott, USA (1986). Sigourney's hot, but hotter still is Jenette Goldstein as Private Vasquez. When one of the male cadets hassles her about her butchness, asking, "Have you ever been mistaken for a man?" she responds simply, "No, have you?"

• Linda Hamilton in *Terminator 2;* James Cameron, USA (1992).

## "So, Which One of You Is the Man?" Butch Lesbians in Mainstream Lesbian-Relationship Films

• Patrice Donnelly. *Personal Best;* Robert Towne, USA (1982). The lesbianism of Mariel (femme) Hemingway's character is treated as a phase (she goes off with a male water-polo player in the end). Patrice Donnelly's character is the "real" lesbian—basic butch. Good butch dialogue. In response to

Hemingway's reluctance to define the true nature of their relationship, Donnelly says, "We may be friends, but we also happen to fuck each other every once in a while." And on meeting Hemingway's new boyfriend: "He's pretty cute for a guy." A memorable love scene, consisting of tickling and nervous giggling and Mariel Hemingway saying, "This isn't so bad, I kind of like this."

•Jane Hallaren in John Sayles's *Lianna,* (1983). Barely butch.

•Beryl Reid in Robert Aldrich's *The Killing of Sister George,* England (1968). Late sixties British butch.

•Anne Heywood in Mark Rydell's *The Fox,* USA (1968). Femmey-butch. Very sexy in and out of her hunting outfit. A truly awful film.

## Butch Lesbians in Independent Lesbian-Themed Films

•Patricia Charbonneau in *Desert Hearts;* Donna Deitch, USA (1986). Sort of butch, butchier than Helen Shaver. Good butch dialogue: "Take your hands out of your pockets and come here."

•Sheila Dabney in *She Must Be Seeing Things;* Sheila McLaughlin, USA (1987). Overly ambitious at times, this feature is notable for its treatment of the explicitly butch/femme relationship between Agatha and Jo.

•Linda Basset in *Waiting for the Moon;* Jill Godmilow USA (1987). Basset plays butch Gertrude Stein opposite Linda Hunt's brilliant Alice B. Toklas.

Also see:

•k.d. lang in *Salmonberries;* Percy Adlon, Germany (1992). *Salmonberries* portrays the developing emotional bonds between two women of very different backgrounds.

Roswitha (Rosel Zech), a librarian in the small Alaskan mining town of Kotzebue, resists lang's affections throughout the film. lang's determined courting climaxes in a tremendous tease of a love scene (or, not a love scene). lang's abilities as an actress are difficult to determine. She doesn't talk much, and she's so captivating when she's on-screen that it's hard to care whether she can act or is just being herself. Whichever, she gives a hot cinematic rendering of a strong, silent, butch dyke in love.

### Cyberdyke (Postmodern Butch)

•Angela Hans Scheirl. *Flaming Ears;* Angela Hans Scheirl, Dietmar Schipek and Ursula Purrer, Austria (1992). As the sullen necrophiliac cyborg, Scheirl wanders the streets reciting some of the most poetically romantic (butch loner) monologues ever written. She's tall, lean, dirty, and handsome in her red PVC coveralls. The sweet tenderness in her puppylike devotion to her new lover's corpse is an inspiring piece of postmodern butch.

### Butch Behind the Camera

•Dorothy Arzner, openly lesbian Hollywood director of the 1930s. In October 1936, *Time* magazine described her as "short, stocky, with a quiet executive manner, a boyish bob and an interest in medicine and sunsets." Her unique sensibility shines through in such classics as *Christopher Strong* (1933), *Craig's Wife* (1936), and *Dance, Girl, Dance* (1940).

**A Sampling of Contemporary Short Films and Videos
Dealing with Butchness, Gender Identity, Masculinity
and Female-to-Male Transgender Issues**

*Brown Sugar Licks Snow White;* Suzi Silbar and Robin
Vachal, USA (1992), 4 mins B&W. [video source; Video
Data Bank] Snippets of voice, text, and image scan the ter-
rain of race and gender, with porno dialogue and girls in
femme drag.

*Dual of the Senses;* Heidi Arnesen, USA (1991), 3 mins. B&W
[16mm source: Frameline] Girl dresses up as boy to do it
with boy dressed up as girl.

*F2M;* Cayte Latta, Australia (1992), 15 mins. [video source:
Australian Film Commission] Interview with Jasper, a
thirty-year-old lesbian female-to-male pre-op transsexual.

*It Wasn't Love;* Sadie Benning, USA (1992), 20 mins. [video
source; Video Data Bank] Sadie does her Fats Domino
impression, sucks her thumb, tells a story about her girlie,
and smiles sweetly for the camera.

*Juggling Gender;* Tami Gold, USA (1992), 27 mins. [video
source: Women Make Movies] A lesbian performance artist
talks about growing up, coming out, lesbian feminism,
and having a beard.

*Linda/Les and Annie;* Annie Sprinkle, Al Jacoma, Johnny
Armstrong, USA (1989), 28 mins. [video source: Annie
Sprinkle] Transsexual Les Nichols and Annie Sprinkle
talk about Les's operation and life, and then fuck with
Les's prosthesis.

*Max;* Monika Treut, USA/Germany (1992), 20 mins. [16mm
source: Frameline]. Female-to-male transsexual Max
Valerio talks about his life and the experience of becoming a man.

*Passing*; Sara Whiteley, USA (1991), 3 mins. 16mm B&W
[16mm source: Frameline] A woman is made over to a
masculine—and then a feminine—extreme.

*P[l]ain Truth;* Ilppo Pohjola, Finland (1993), 15 mins. [35mm
source: Zeitgeist Films] A painful and cathartic "symbolic documentary" based on the experience of Rudi, a
female-to-male transsexual.

*Stafford's Story;* Susan Muska, USA (1992), 3 mins. [video
source: Frameline]. Stafford tells about an encounter at
a sex club.

*Storme: The Lady of the Jewel Box;* Michelle Parkerson,
USA (1987), 21 mins. [16mm source: Women Make
Movies]. An overview of the career of the famous black
male impersonator, Storme DeLarverie.

### Index of Feature Titles (with sources):

*Aliens* [Films Inc.]
*Blue Steel* [Swank]
*Calamity Jane* [Kit Parker Films]
*Desert Hearts* [Samuel Goldwyn]
*Desperate Living* [Films Inc.]
*Flaming Ears* [Women Make Movies]
*The Fox* [Films Inc.]
*The Killing of Sister George* [Films Inc.]
*Lianna* [Swank]
*Liquid Sky* [New Yorker]
*A Man Like Eva* [New Yorker]
*Personal Best* [Swank]
*Queen Christina* [Swank]
*Seven Women* [Films Inc.]
*She Must Be Seeing Things* [First Run Features]
*Silence of the Lambs* [Swank]
*Something Special* [Cori International]
*Some Kind of Wonderful* [Films Inc.]
*Sullivan's Travels* [Swank]
*Summer Vacation: 1999* [New Yorker]
*Switch* [Swank]
*Times Square* [Swank]
*Touch of Evil* [Swank]
*Turnabout* [Budget]
*Vera* [Kino International]
*Victor/Victoria* [Swank]
*Virgina* [Mercure Distribution]
*Virgin Machine* [First Run Features]
*Waiting for the Moon* [Samuel Goldwyn]
*Yentl* [Swank]
*Yiddle with His Fiddle* [Em Gee Film Library/Brandeis
    University]

## Film and Video Exhibition Sources

Australian Film Commission, (612) 925-7333

Brandeis University—National Center for Jewish Film, (617) 899-7044

Cori International, 2049 Century Park East, #780, Los Angeles, CA 90067 (310) 557-0173

Em Gee Film Library, 6924 Canby Avenue, Suite 102, Reseda, CA 91335 (818) 981-5506

Films Inc., 5547 North Ravenswood Avenue, Chicago, IL 60640 (800) 323-4222, Ext. 42

First Run Features, 153 Waverly Place, New York, NY 10018 (212) 243-0600

Frameline, 346 Ninth St., San Francisco, CA 94103 (415) 703-8650

Kino International, 333 West 39th Street, Suite 503, New York, NY 10018 (212) 629-6880

Kit Parker Films, 1245 Tenth Street, Monterey, CA 93940 (800) 538-5838

Mercure Distribution, FAX (33-1) 45-65-07-47

New Yorker Films, 16 West 61st Street, New York, NY 10023 (212) 247-6110

Samuel Goldwyn Co., 10203 Santa Monica Boulevard, #500, Los Angeles, Ca 90067 (310) 552-2255

Annie Sprinkle, P.O. Box 1024, Long Island City, NY 11101

Swank, 201 South Jefferson/P.O. Box 231, St. Louis, MO 63166 (800) 876-5577

Tara Releasing, 124 Belvedere, #5, San Rafael, CA 94901 (415) 454-5838

Video Data Bank, 32 South Wabash Avenue, Chicago, IL 60603 (312) 899-5172

Women Make Movies, 225 Lafayette Street, #206, New York, NY 10012 (212) 925-0606

Zeitgeist Films, 200 Waverly Place, #4, New York, NY 10014 (212) 727-1989

## Contact Sources for Video Rental and Purchase

Charis Video, P.O. Box 797, Brooklyn, NY 11231

Facets Multimedia, 1517 West Fullerton Avenue, Chicago, IL 60614 (800) 331-6197

Lambda Rising, 1625 Connecticut Avenue NW, Washington DC 20009 (202) 462-6969

TLA Video, 332 South Street, Philadelphia, PA 19147 (215) 922-1014

RANDY TUROFF
# Chic by Nature (a work in progress)

### I. Lesbian Transgender

In the privacy of the bedroom, she stands in front of the full-length mirror and applies mascara to the fine hair along the sides of her face. She cocks the black fedora and turns the brim down. Tonight she's going out on the town—the town of San Francisco, where private fantasies are accessible and acceptable in sectors of the public domain.

The mascara hardens on her face and the hairs stand on end, but they're too dark and smudgy. Rummaging through the drawer, she finds two handmade human hair mustaches which had been stowed away after Joe, Jim, Kurt, and Marc died, after the theater circle disappeared through attrition. The spirit gum in the bottle has thickened, but is still usable. One of the mustaches is flaxen blond. It won't do. The other is mottled blondish with auburn overtones and grayish grizzle from too many color changes. It's perfect for her now as a youthful mid-age lesbian man-about-town.

The first international S.F. drag king contest is happening at The Eagle, a gay male leather bar. She used to wear black leather and go there to watch leathermen and drag-queen contests with gay theater buddies, eight or nine years ago. They're all dead now. She looks like they would have then—it's her homage to them and to a younger self still alive after all these years. Tonight she resurrects her butch-drag persona. But this time it's in the company of lesbians. Time is finally on her side.

Sabrina is standing in the shadows outside the bar, talking to friends. Sabrina's a gay man who does lesbian drag—a colleague at the newspaper. Sabrina doesn't recognize her at first. "Fab-u-lous. You're fabulous," s/he croons. "Shall I still call you Randy?" What else? "I received my stage name in the womb."

The place is packed, packed with women. Video cameras, lights, and throngs of friends encourage me toward the room backstage. The girls are making adjustments and sizing up the competition. Elvis Herselvis is M.C. I hear her bellow: "And Here Comes Randy," and in an instant I find myself strutting across the huge platform stage with cameras rolling and hundreds of people cheering as the array of drag-king characters suddenly come to life under the lights and eyes and smiles of a wildly appreciative audience!

As a lesbian-identified female, I've wondered about my male personas. How do they fit into my eroticism? How does my gender affect my sexuality? How do my gender affectations jibe with my sexual orientation? What do I like about lesbian sex?

Starting with the mustache, I think of what it does for me.

It gives me a stiff upper lip. I feel constrained when I smile. I like that. I like the control over my emotions—the consciousness of constrained movement. I'm constantly reminded of gender as a role. The mustache is also a metaphor, a shield protecting the vulnerability of my mouth and lips—my vulva. At rest, in or out of costume, I prefer to sit with my legs spread, my chest open, and the length of my arm extended along the length of a sofa. I'm rather androgynous. But I never feel at ease in femme drag. The constraints of femme role-playing don't please me. They make me feel vulnerable and disempowered.

My sex partner is comfortable in femme drag. She paints her lips, highlights her eyes and has long hair, all of which accentuate her movements which are precisely seductive. She makes herself visible. The way she protects herself is by directing, modulating, accepting or rejecting the gaze of the other towards her. In her dress, I can see her legs and some of her thigh. I can see the shape of her waist, the movement of her hips, and the accurate suggestion of the shape and size of her breasts.

When I undress her, removing her bra, her warm flesh moves with expectation in my hands. Her pubic hair is pressed beneath black lace, waiting to be released. I love to release her. I love her vulnerability and deference. And yet, when the sex act is under way, the ritualized roles often change—the dance takes its own turns, according to more spontaneous desires. Free of constraint of role or of clothing, we do what we want.

Sometimes she fucks me the way men have fucked her in ways she's liked. I can share the enjoyment because it's been filtered and reconstituted as female sex expressed as lesbian desire. I also like to take her from behind, boy on boy.

Very kiki. For me, lesbian sex is transgendered and inclusive. In bed, sharing our sexual expertise and a lifetime of desires and fantasies, we can become a veritable universe of possibilities.

Looking once again in the mirror, she sees her female body, but is not turned on. She has nice breasts, fine skin, and a pleasing shape, but she focuses on the tattoo —that is what pleases her the most.

What is it about desire which makes me ecstatic about another woman's body which in essence is not so different from my own? Why is desire so precise? I can go to a public bathhouse and see many female bodies, all the variations, but rarely do I feel erotic attraction—it's more like looking in the mirror. For me, lesbianism is not narcissism. And yet sometimes something happens and my urges surge and inflame me. I could make love to a stranger on the spot who happens to move her knee in a way I can't ignore. My eyes give me away, and that's how the conversation usually starts and ends. Whether I take the risk, act on the fantasy or not, usually depends upon reciprocity. My female intuition leads me on, either seducing me to action or to writing about that which is better off left as literature, as a reflection of my own desire.

## II. Forbidden Zone

Language can't just slide over this pain.

The plunge is necessarily vertical, off the cliff into biographical data, extrafilmic material, ravines of deep symbolism. It's into the land of hungry ghosts with tattoos in the wrong places—visible, making them apparently unemployable beneath the corporate code into the under-class whose mantra of race, class, gender, race, class, gender echoes to the glass ceiling and falls back recycled by generations and regenerations of those left outside the profit margin.

I'm reading a batch of books I'm assigned to review. I just broke up with my lover of six years. Every book seems to exhibit a wicked synchronicity with which a turn of phrase leads me directly to thoughts of her which sends me lost through the jungle of thorns until I'm too messy, bled, and spent to make it to the next chapter.

Like this quote in Terry Castle's *The Apparitional Lesbian* taken from Henry James's *The Bostonians*: "Olive's fright-ful wrenching sobs convey only a wild personal passion, a desire to take her friend in her arms again on any terms, even the most cruel to herself."

And then it happens: the tug-of-love war starts pulling me apart. The book gets earmarked, and Diamanda Galas makes an appearance on my VCR wringing out every ounce of pain from Billie Holiday's "Gloomy Sunday." It's the sudden and total collapse of reason into the black hole. And "if I should take the notion to jump in the ocean, ain't nobody's business if I do." But she didn't. She took vacations instead. Left her mind, shut the door, and went on heroin holiday from herself. But you can't live there, Billie Holiday. And there "was a time I was [her] only one. But now, I'm the sad and lonely one, lordy. Was I gay, till today? Now she's gone and we're through, am I blue?"

Do we use black people to weep for us? asks Minnie Bruce Pratt. I was previewing films for an upcoming festival. There was a music video of one old black blues man singing about hard times and depression in the Delta. My African-

American colleagues say fast-forward this...it's slave music.

I hate to admit it but I'm someone who has worshipped in the dungeons as well as the churches, giving everything up to God and witnessing stigmata of passion bleeding on surfaces of flesh left as graffiti, or tattoos, or inscriptions in cement: "Randy loves Katie."

In her latest book (*What I Found There*), Adrienne Rich quotes from a review of an anthology of sixty Los Angeles poets. "The book is not a response to public life,...it speaks of art as mere self-disclosure: we tell about our troubles, and we feel better." Rich asks: "Who is to dictate what may be written about and how?" But she also sees the finger pointing at that reality which looms large on the satellite dish where violent crimes are captured on home video and projected globally. Misery talks incessantly, vying for most victimized, kinkiest, and most oppressed. It's somebody's yesterday, trauma-packed, frozen as content, and produced by those who don't believe or understand a word of it.

So I'm swinging down today into a silence, a land I've known—that place beneath the stage, behind the scenes, tossed on the cutting-room floor, unsaved, undocumented and not open to public scrutiny. It's pre-narrative, post-structural, and neither here nor there, neither this nor that. My self without you, without my self.

### III. Rites of Passage

Judy Grahn writes that most stories are descent stories, featuring a crisis leading to transformation.

I'm searching for this rite of passage—this new declaration of independence, not defined by loss or invisibility.

A way to surface somehow with integrity through
a channel which leads to
available power
on a personal basis
which, of course, becomes political:
how to make the power available.

In my dream, there was a double-headed snake, guarding
the dualities. The primal act of courage was decapitation,
like Kali using the double-edged sword to sever her own
head, ego dripping blood. For it is the ego which holds onto
the fears, the fears engendered by binary opposition:

To have, or have not

To be, or not to be

To be on-line or off-line and down and out of it—divinely
mad.

I'm looking for fuller disclosure, more understanding, not
more codification or mediation by alias digitation, but
more embodiment of virtual possibilities. The reconstruction after the deconstruction. The heightened flavors,
tastes, moods, and emotions. The power of it. The lesbian
body of it.

But do we really have to go all the way back to our ances-
tral brain stems, all the way back to the Snake Goddess
herself to reclaim our power, to reclaim the external phallus as the original internalized vagina? Do we need to invoke
the maternal birth canal like some ancient form of feminist alchemy, in order to bring our bodies back home from
the labs and breakdown lanes on the communication highway? Can we reimagine gender without procreation and
without losing our wombs in transit?

Do certain metaphors translate power into physical form? as Judy Grahn predicates.

And why is it true that lesbian feminist authority is still the biggest taboo?—Adrienne Rich.

Is it really certain that the masters' tools will never dismantle the masters' house, as Audre Lorde wrote?

Are we being stuck once again in roles not of our choosing? Do we really need to be sold back to ourselves as bisexual-ized Madonnas or as Mrs. Hundred-Dollar-a-Plate Homosexuals before we buy into the notion of our own worth?

We do seem to have lost the knack for being chic by nature.

On the other hand, aren't we getting there as we speak, as we write ourselves into the world at large, demanding dialogue.

I'm putting politics aside for now and switching channels, moving into my own movie. Once again I'm in bed, naked with you, in love and wild. Perhaps this has always been the sacred space of transformation for me. There are poems to prove it. It's *always* love, no matter how fleeting, no matter how it turns out. Service or surrender, it's the yoga of the dying world full of life and dying alive.

I'm splitting the screen with Isaac Julien's film, *Looking for Langston*. The voice-over belongs to the poet Essex Hemphill: "Love is a dangerous word in this small town. Those who seek it are sometimes found facedown floating on their beds. Those who find it protect it or destroy it from within..."

And yes, I will remember your beauty, long after you've forgotten it. And so it's back full cycle to us again, whichever "us," to the creation and destruction and re-creation, and recreation and the next party after the next funeral. It's *always* Kali, stepping on two fornicating bodies, the bloody smile lingering on her severed head.

### IV. Black and Blonde

A woman at the bar comes up to me and asks, Are you pure white or part native American? with the emphasis on "pure." I look at her, she says, I'm Filipino-Mexican. Very California, I answer. Sorry she says I didn't mean to offend you. God, I thought, I don't *dance* like a Nazi.

In *The Last Generation,* Cherrie Moraga writes: "I have never had a race-less relationship. Somehow I have always attributed this to being mixed-blood, but I wonder if anyone has. Maybe white people are the only ones in this country to enjoy the luxury of being 'colorblind' with one another."

In a far-off kingdom, long ago, in a culturally defined tribal setting, two women fell in love. One had bigger breasts than the other, and the other had curlier hair. They were both shades of white. They fetishized their differences and had great sex together. Eventually they were persecuted; not for being lesbians but for refusing to marry men and be mothers.

Essex Hemphill asks, "Does Your Mama Know about Me?" in an essay on Robert Mapplethorpe after the photo "Man in a Polyester Suit," you know, the one with the huge black dick hanging out of the pants. Hemphill calls Mapplethorpe on it, saying that the photo is really "Black Dick in a Polyester Suit" and that it's a case of classic sexual exploitation and racial objectification.

In the essay "Skin Head Sex Thing" critic Kobena Mercer talks about negrophilia and the allegations of "othering" against Mapplethorpe. He goes along with it until, bam, he turns the beat around and goes—No—this is logical slippage—No, I will not identify with the objectification of the Negro, just because I'm black. Fetishism is not necessarily a bad thing.

I agree—fetishism among friends can be fun. Mapplethorpe himself agreed: "I was part of it," he said in an interview. "People in the photos were friends of mine. They trusted me." I believe him, I mean how can you deny the credentials of a man with a bullwhip up his ass? Picking on Mapplethorpe is a dangerous call; it can easily backfire, turn Right, and blow us all out of the water. I say look to the horizon and see the coming and coming out of all the new colonialists who need us for market and material. The salient question is: who makes the profit, who's profiteering, and who's a false prophet?

The film critic Richard Dyer writes: "How we are seen determines in part how we are treated." And "How we treat others is based on how we see them."

But how do we see ourselves? In unity? In diversity? In macro and micro community? How porous can we be and still maintain homoerotic identity?

I had a girlfriend once, who was the perfect manifestation of the blonde sex goddess, the blonde goddess of the late-late-night movie reruns of my formative years. She wasn't a porn star, and she wasn't on MTV, but she was a prototypical cultural icon of desirability—mostly because she looked and dressed the part and played the role so well. In effect, she was objectified by consent. In truth, she was no more high femme than she was heterosexual. Like the black man in the polyester suit, she had the stuff and flaunted it.

The moral of this political narrative is that perhaps we're

all guilty of wanting to be loved for the illusions we create, both to attract others and to keep ourselves hidden.

And why shouldn't all of us have equal opportunity to be less than who we really are, to fulfill some bartered fantasy? Why not give everybody access to glamour lighting. If women want to appropriate the gestures and costumes of the boys in charge—give them equal opportunity. If people of color want to be make-believe white in a make-believe ballroom, in *Paris Is Burning,* so be it.

But this is a cautionary tale. One of the fastest ways to lose personal power has always been to deny the versions of where and how you've lived and been known. Assimilated communities give up the power to reinvent themselves at will. They lose the know-how along with their characters. Their stories become bland and repressed.

I'll take Monique Wittig's (abridged) political definition of homosexuality, as a workable guideline: love, same-sex, and against the norm. I like it because it's flexible enough for me to be able to change my mind. I'd also add a fillip for those who are phase-spacing or in transit: Welcome to homo homeland, the ever-evolving queer zone.

## Works Cited

Castle, Terry. *The Apparitional Lesbian.* Columbia University Press, 1993.

Dyer, Richard. *The Matter of Images.* Routledge, 1993.

Grahn, Judy. *Blood, Bread, and Roses.* Beacon, 1993.

Hemphill, Essex. *Ceremonies.* Plume, 1992.

Julien, Isaac, director. *Looking for Langston,* 1988 film.

Livingston, Jennie, director. *Paris Is Burning,* 1990 film.

Lorde, Audre. *Sister Outsider.* Crossing Press, 1984.

Mapplethorpe, Robert. "Man in a Polyester Suit," 1980 photograph.

Mercer, Kobena. "Skin Head Sex Thing" in the anthology *How Do I Look?* ed. by Bad Object-Choices. Bay Press, 1991.

Moraga, Cherrie. *The Last Generation.* South End Press, 1993.

Pratt, Minnie Bruce. *Rebellion: Essays 1980–91.* Firebrand, 1991.

Rich, Adrienne. *What Is Found There.* Norton, 1993.

JUDITH HALBERSTAM
# F2M: The Making of Female Masculinity

This essay will call for new sexual vocabularies that acknowledge sexualities and genders as styles rather than simply lifestyles, as fictions rather than the basic facts of life and as potentialities rather than as fixed identities. It will also ask how and in what ways does the disintegration and reconsitution of gender identities focus upon the postmodern lesbian body? And further, what is postmodern about lesbian identity?

In the 1990s, lesbian communities have witnessed an unprecedented proliferation in sexual practices or at least in the open discussion of lesbian practices. Magazines like *Outlook* and *On Our Backs* have documented ongoing debates about gender, sexuality, and venues for sexual play, and even mainstream cinema has picked up on a new visibility of lesbian identities (*Basic Instinct* [1992] for example). Lesbians are particularly invested in proliferating their identities and practices because, as the sex debates of the 1980s demonstrated, policing activity within the community and commitment to a unitary conception of lesbianism has had some very negative and problematic repercussions.[1]

Some queer identities have appeared recently in lesbian zines and elsewhere: Guys with pussies, dykes with dicks, queer butches, aggressive femmes, F2Ms, lesbians who like men, daddy boys, gender queens, drag kings, pomo afro homos, bulldaggers, women who fuck boys, women who fuck like boys, dyke mommies, transsexual lesbians, male lesbians. As the list suggests, gay/lesbian/straight simply cannot account for the range of sexual experience available. In this essay, I hone in on the female-to-male transsexual and I argue that within a more general fragmentation of the concept of sexual identity, the specificity of the transsexual disappears. In a way, I claim, we are all transgendered.

We are all transgenders except that the referent of the "trans" becomes less and less clear (and more and more queer). We are all cross-dressers but where are we crossing from, and to what? There is no "other" side, no "opposite" sex, no natural divide to be spanned by surgery, by disguise, by passing. We all pass or we don't, we all wear our drag, and we all derive a different degree of pleasure— sexual or otherwise—from our costumes. It is just that for some our costumes are made of fabric or material, while for others they are made of skin; for some an outfit can be changed, for others skin must be resewn. There are no transsexuals.

Desire has a terrifying precision. Pleasure might be sex with a woman who looks like a boy; pleasure might be a woman going in disguise as a man to a gay bar in order to pick up a gay man; pleasure might be two naked women; pleasure might be masturbation watched by a stranger; pleasure might be a man and a woman; but pleasure seems to be precise. In an interview with a pre-op female-to-male transsexual called Danny, Chris Martin asks Danny about his very particular desire to have sex with men as a man. "What's the difference," she asks, "between having sex with men now and having sex with men before?" Danny responds: "I didn't really. If I did, it was oral sex…it was already gay sex…umm…that was a new area. It depends upon your partner's perception. If a man thought I was a woman, we didn't do it."[2] Danny requires that his partners recognize that he is a man before he has "gay" sex with them. He demands that they read his gender accurately according to his desire, in other words; though, he admits, there is room for the occasional misreading. On one occasion, for example, he recalls that a trick he had picked up discovered that Danny did not have a penis. Danny allowed his partner to penetrate him vaginally because "It was what he had been looking for all his life, only he hadn't realized it. When he saw me, it was like 'Wow. I want a man with a vagina.'"

Wanting a man with a vagina, or wanting to be a woman transformed into a man having sex with other men are fairly precise and readable desires, precise and yet not at all represented by the categories for sexual identity that we have settled for. And, as another pre-op female-to-male transsexual, Vern, makes clear, the so-called gender community is often excluded by or vilified by the gay community. Vern calls it "genderphobia":

"Genderphobia" is my term. I made it up because there is a clone movement in the non-heterosexual community to make everybody look just like heterosexuals who sleep with each other. The fact is that there is a whole large section of the gay community who is going to vote Republican...[3]

Genderphobia, as Vern suggests, indicates all kind of gender trouble in the mainstream gay and lesbian community. Furthermore, the increasing numbers of female-to-male transsexuals (f-to-m's) appearing in, particularly, metropolitan or urban lesbian communities has given rise to interesting and sometimes volatile debates among lesbians about f-to-m's.[4]

Genderbending among lesbians is not limited to sex-change operations. In New York, sex queen Annie Sprinkle has been running "Drag King for a Day" workshops with pre-op f-to-m Jack Armstrong, a long-time gender activist. The workshops instruct women in the art of passing and culminate in a night out on the town as men. Alisa Solomon wrote about her experience in the workshop for the *Village Voice*. Solomon reports how eleven women flattened their breasts, donned strips of stage makeup facial hair, "loosened our belts a notch to make our waistlines fall, pulled back hair, put on vests."[5] Solomon felt inclined, however, to draw the line at putting a sock in her Jockeys because she was interested in gender, not sex. A penis has nothing to do with it." She also notes in response to Jack Armstrong's discussion of his transsexuality: "I could have done without his photo-aided descriptions of phalloplasties and other surgical procedures. After all I had no interest in how to *be* a man; I only wanted, for the day, to be *like* one."

Solomon's problematic response to the issue of transsexualism is indicative of the way that many lesbians embrace the idea of gender performance, but they reduce it to just that, an act with no relation to biology, real or imagined. Solomon disavows the penis here as if that alone is the mark of gender—she is comfortable with the clothes, the false facial hair, but the suggestion of a constructed penis leads her to make an essential difference between feigning maleness for a day and being a man. In fact, as she wanders off into the Village in her drag, Alisa Solomon, inasmuch as she passes successfully, *is* a man, is male, is a man for a day. The insistence here that the penis alone signifies maleness, corresponds to a tendency within academic discussions of gender to continue to equate masculinity solely with men. Recent studies on masculinity[6] persist in making masculinity an extension or discursive effect of maleness. But what about female masculinity or lesbian masculinity?

In the introduction to her ground-breaking new study of transvestism, *Vested Interests,*[7] Marjorie Garber discusses the ways that transvestism and transsexualism provoke a "category crisis." Garber elaborates this term, suggesting that often the crisis occurs elsewhere but is displaced onto the ambiguity of gender. Solomon obviously confronts a "category crisis" as she ponders the politics of stuffing her Jockeys, and presumably such a crisis is one of the intended by-products of Sprinkle/Armstrong's workshop. Solomon attempts to resolve her category crisis by assuring herself that she wants to look *like* a man not *be* a man and that therefore her desire has nothing to do with possession of the penis. But in fact, what Solomon misunderstands is that penises as well as masculinity become artificial and constructable when we challenge the naturalness of gender. Socks in genetic girls' Jockeys are part and parcel of creating fictitious genders; they are not reducible to sex.

But what then is the significance of the surgically constructed penis in this masquerade of sex and gender? In the chapter of her study called "Spare Parts: The Surgical Construction of Gender," Garber discusses the way that the phenomenon of transsexuality "demonstrates that essentialism *is* cultural construction."[8] She suggests that f-to-m surgery has been less common and less studied than male-to-female transsexual operations partly because medical technology has not been able to construct a functional penis, but also on account of "a sneaking feeling that it should not be so easy to "construct" a "man"—which is to say, a male body." (102). Garber is absolutely right, I think, to draw attention to a kind of conscious or unconscious unwillingness within the medical establishment to explore the options for f-to-m surgery. After all, the construction of a functional penis for f-to-m transsexuals could alter inestimably the most cherished fictions of gender in the Western world.

If penises were purchasable, functional penises in other words, who exactly might want one? What might the effect of surgically produced penises be upon notions like "penis envy," "castration complex," "size queens"? If anyone could have one, who would want one? How would the power relations of gender be altered by a market for the penis? Who might want a bigger one? Who might want an artificial one rather than the "natural" one they were born with? What if surgically constructed models "work" better? Can the penis be improved upon? Certainly the folks at Good Vibrations, who have been in the business of selling silicone dildos for years now, could tell you about many models as good as, if not better than, the "real" thing.

Obviously, the potential of medical technology to alter bodies makes natural gender and biological sex merely antiquated categories in the history of sexuality, part, in other words, of the inventedness of sex. Are we then, as Jan Morris claims in her autobiography *Conundrum: An Extraordinary Narrative of Transsexualism,* possibly entering a post-transsexual era?[9] I believe we are occupying the transition here and now, that we are experiencing a boundary change, a shifting of focus that may have begun with the invention of homosexuality at the end of the nineteenth century, but that will end with the invention of the sexual body at the end of the twentieth century. Which does not mean that we will all in some way surgically alter our bodies, it means that we will begin to acknowledge the ways in which we have already surgically, technologically, and ideologically altered our bodies, our identities, ourselves.

One might expect, then, in these postmodern times that as we posit the artificiality of gender and sex with increasing awareness of how and why our bodies have been policed into gender identities, there might be a decrease in the incidence of such things as sex-change operations. On the contrary, however, especially in lesbian circles (and it is female-to-male transsexualism that I am concerned with here) there has been, as I suggested, a rise in discussions of, depictions of and requests for f-to-m sex change operations.

While I want to avoid the inevitable binarism of a debate about whether transsexual operations are redundant, I do think that the terms in which we have inherited from medicine to think through transsexualism, sex changes, and sexual surgery must change. Just as the idea of crossdressing presumes an immutable line between two opposite sexes, so transsexualism, as a term, as an ideology, presumes that if you are not one you are the other. I propose that we call all elective body alterations for whatever reason (post-cancer or post-accident reconstruction, physical disabilities, or gender dysphoria) cosmetic surgery and that we drop altogether the constrictive terminology of crossing.[10]

An example from a recent series on plastic surgery in the *Los Angeles Times* may illustrate my point. The series, titled "The Revolution in Cosmetic Surgery," covers the pros and cons of the plastic-surgery industry. By way of making a point about the interdependence of the business of cosmetic surgery and the fashion industry, the writer states the obvious: namely, that very often media standards for beauty impose a "world-wide standard of beauty" that lead non-Western, nonwhite women to desire the "eyes, cheekbones, or breasts of their favorite North American television star."[11] By way of illustrating his point, Scheer suggests that "turning a Japanese housewife...into a typical product of the dominant white American genetic mix—for whatever that is worth—is now eminently do-able." He quotes from an Asian woman who says she wants to be like an American, "You know. Big eyes. Everybody, all my girlfriends did their eyes deeper, so I did." Scheer asks her what is next on her cosmetic surgery agenda: "Nose and chin this time around." Scheer comments:

> Eyelids are often redone too. Asian women don't have a crease in the middle. Why does one need an extra fold like two tracks running horizontally across the eyelid? Why is the smooth expanse of eyelid skin not perfect enough? The answer is that the desirable eye, the one extolled in the massive cosmetic industry blitz campaigns, is the Western eye, and the two lines provide the border for eye shadow and other makeup applications.

Scheer's rhetorical question as to why "the smooth expanse

of eyelid skin" is not acceptable is supposed to ironize the relationship between body politics and market demands. His answer to his own question is to resolve that the dictates of the marketplace govern seemingly aesthetic considerations. And, we might add, the racially marked face is not only marginalized by a kind of economy of beauty, it is also quite obviously the product of imperialist, sexist, and racist ideologies. The cosmetic production of occidental beauty in this scene of cosmetic intervention, then, certainly ups the ante on racist and imperialist notions of aesthetics, but it also has the possibly unforeseen effect of making race obviously artificial, another fiction of culture.

Cosmetic surgery, then, can, in a sometimes contradictory way, both bolster dominant ideologies of beauty and power and it can undermine completely the fixedness of race, class, and gender by making each one surgically or sartorially reproducible. By commenting only upon the racist implications of such surgery in his article, Scheer has sidestepped the constructedness of race altogether. To all intents and purposes, if we are to employ the same rhetoric that pertains to transsexualism, the Japanese woman paying for the face job has had a race change (and here we might also think of the surgical contortions of Michael Jackson). She has altered her appearance until she appears to be white.

Why, then, do we not mark surgery that focuses on racial features in the same way that we positively pathologize surgery that alters the genitals? In "Spare Parts," Marjorie Garber makes a similar point:

Why does a "nose job" or "breast job" or "eye job" pass as mere self-improvement, all—as the word "job" implies—in a day's work for a surgeon (or an actress), while a sex change (could we imagine it called a "penis job"?) represents the dislocation of everything we conventionally "know" or believe about gender identities and gender roles, "male" and "female" subjectivities?[12]

The rhetoric of cosmetic surgery, in other words, reveals that identity is nowhere more obviously bound to gender and sexuality than in the case of transsexual surgery. And gender and sexuality are nowhere more obviously hemmed in by binary options.

Transsexual lesbian playwright Kate Bornstein perhaps phrases it best in her latest theater piece, which is called *The Opposite Sex Is Neither*. Describing herself as a "gender outlaw," Bornstein writes:

See, I'm told I must be a man or a woman. One or the other. Oh, it's OK to be a transsexual, say some—just don't talk about it. Don't question your gender any more, just be a woman now—you went to so much trouble—just be satisfied. I am not so satisfied.[13]

As a gender outlaw, Bornstein gives gender a new context, a new definition. She demands that her audience read her not as man or woman, or lesbian or heterosexual, but as some combination of presumably incompatible terms.

In a video documenting the first experience of sexual intercourse by a new f-to-m transsexual, Annie Sprinkle introduces the viewers to the world of f-to-m sex changes. The video *Linda / Les and Annie* is remarkable as a kind of post-op, post-porn, postmodern artifact of what Sprinkle calls "gender flexibility." It is archaic, however, in its tendency to fundamentally realign sex and gender. In the video, Les Nichols, a post-op f-to-m transsexual, sexually experiments with his new surgically constructed penis. The video records the failure of Les's first attempt at intercourse as a "man" and yet it celebrates the success of his gender flexibility. In *Linda/Les, and Annie,* Les Nichols talks about *his* new gender identity not in terms of being an outlaw but in a rather simple series of reversals. Where once Les was a radical lesbian feminist who attacked a system built around male privilege, now Les claims that one of the most pleasurable experiences he has had in his new body is the automatic and immediate respect he receives simply because people perceive him as a man. The video alternates between three modes of representation: a sentimentalized fiction of new love between Les and Annie, a graphic depiction of sex between Les and Annie and, finally, a pseudo-documentary-style interview with Les. It is in this last mode that Les is almost offensive in his glorification of the male mystique.

By apparently understanding his gender performance as no performance at all and his gender fiction as the straight-up truth, Les Nichols takes the trans out of transsexualism. There is no movement, or only a very limited and fleeting movement, in crossing from a stable female identity to a stable male identity, and Les seems not to challenge notions of natural gender at all. Indeed his self-presentation simply employs the reductive rhetoric of inversion that suggests that one true identity hides within an other waiting for an opportunity to emerge.

However, what I have called the post-pornographic scenes of the video do undermine somewhat Les's totalized and seamless self-presentation. The sex scenes are "post-pornographic" in that not only do they show everything, they show more than everything. Not only do we see the phallus, but we see its constructedness; not only do we witness the sex act, but we see its failure and then its simulation and ad-libbed imperfection. The sex between Les and Annie, much more than Les's discussion of his new gender, makes sexuality into an elaborate and convoluted ritual that strives to match body parts and make complementarity out of some-times-unwilling flesh.

Apart from its appeal to a kind of freakish voyeurism, the sex scene between Les and Annie manages to accomplish what the more factual and explanatory parts of the video could not—it shows the degree of difficulty involved in the sex act, a difficulty that can enhance or diminish pleasure as the case may be, and it oddly but interestingly refocuses the gaze away from Les's transitivity and toward Annie Sprinkle's. It is Annie's body as much as Les's that represents a postmodern lesbian desire in this video, for it is she who most obviously gets off on the spectacle of the female body becoming male. Annie's desire, her ability to be a reader of gender, her titillation and pleasure, are all stimulated by the ambiguity of Les's body parts, by his hermaphroditic genitals, by his sewn and painted skin. Her fantasy, her sexuality, is a part of the enactment of "trans-sex" rather than its object or incidental partner.

Much of the literature on transsexualism pays little or no attention to the desire directed toward the transsexual. While Judith Butler's dictum from *Gender Trouble* that some girls like "their boys to be girls"[14] has been understood widely in terms of a butch-femme aesthetic, it can also apply quite literally to those girls who like their boys to have been genetic girls. As in the earlier example of the man who had been looking all his life for a guy with a pussy, there are some women who have always been searching for a woman with a dick or a dyke with a dick. Annie Sprinkle says that Les is perfect for her because of her own "bisexuality": somehow Les's imperfect masculinity and his possession of penis and clitoris appeal to some very specific phantasmatic projection. While some girls are content with boys who retain genetically female bodies, others desire the transgendered or cosmetically altered body.

Contexts, then, and what I am calling readers of gender fiction, as much as bodies create sexuality and gender and their transitivities. In many situations, gender or gendering takes at least two. By turning to another representation of gender fiction, the film *Vera,* I want to give an example of transgendered desire that does not involve cosmetic body alterations. In so doing, we might ask a question like what is the difference between cross-sexing and cross-dressing in terms of representation and the reading of gender? Or, to what degree is the postmodernity of the lesbian body determined by its will to be gendered? What happens when the gender reader refuses to read? What happens to a gender fiction that is misunderstood? We can also return here to the question of to what extent we live in a post-transsexual era.

Sergio Toledo's film *Vera* explores the intricate story of Vera Bauer's negotiation of her sex and gender contradictions. Vera changes her name to Bauer and begins to dress in drag as she successfully (if temporarily) becomes a man. Bauer, right up until the end of the film, seems satisfied with her creation of a gender fiction—by dressing up in a suit and tie and appearing in public as a man, she lives and owns the particular fiction of her gender. This film, by centering upon a young woman's desire to be a man but avoiding a direct discussion of transsexualism, directs our attention to the complex negotiations that take place between body, sex, and gender to create an experience of dysphoria.

But dysphoria does not always and in every case require surgical intervention in order to be resolved; in fact, dysphoria does not necessarily need to be resolved at all. Indeed, gender dysphoria within lesbian circles is often embraced and channeled within sex play as a libidinal force. In the Los Angeles lesbian zine *Scream Box,* for example, Cathie Opie, a photographer whose work depicts gender ambiguity, challenges readers with a photograph of herself in butch drag. The caption reads: "Your parents should be happy that you have such a man for a girlfriend."[15]

This photograph resonates with a moment from *Vera* when Bauer passes herself off as a very respectable young man to her girlfriend's parents. The parents do not see through Bauer's act even momentarily; there is no double take, no vertiginous refocusing of their expectations. Bauer is a man and Opie is a man, and as each artificially takes on their manhood, they both become more adept at masculinity than most men could hope to be.

*Vera* poses the question of dress and identity in a fascinating way: Vera Bauer is a young woman who refuses to be female. She wraps her breasts and she dresses in a man's suit; she tells her guardian that she has the wrong body. In a relationship that develops between Bauer (as she insists on being called) and another woman, Bauer's lesbianism promises to solve her gender dysphoria. However, in a crucial scene between Bauer and her lover, Bauer discovers that she can no more be a woman for a woman than she could be a woman for a man.

The question posed by this film is whether and how dressing and cross-dressing stabilize or destabilize sexual identity. In *Vera,* Bauer dresses up in a costume in order to hide some supposedly "true" identity but, in fact, as the film progresses the costume becomes equivalent to self. The disguise, in other words, reveals the artificiality of the sexual dress code and at the same time it seems to produce another sexuality, a set of desires previously inaccessible. The cross-dressing sexuality is worn outside the body, like another skin, it replaces anatomy in the chain of signifiers that eventually stabilizes into something like a sexual identity: sexuality in this model is a surface that hides and is hidden, an outfit that covers and lays bare.

Vera Bauer cross-dresses because, as she tells her girlfriend Clara, "I am a man, you know." Bauer and Clara sit across from one another in a dark restaurant; Bauer lip-syncs "I'm Your Man" and defies Clara to contradict her. The lip-synch act replicates perfectly Bauer's gender act, her cross-dressing, transgendered identity; but it also makes a point about Bauer's implicit belief that she is stuck in the wrong body. Lip synching is an act of simulation but is no less real for that; the match between mouthed words and recorded voice, taped music and "live" silence symbolizes the intricate meanings of Bauer's speech act. When Bauer says "I am a man" to her girlfriend, she lip-synchs the masculinity that she both wears and owns.

The tragedy of this film lies not in Bauer's gender confusion, however, but in her girlfriend's inability or unwillingness to read the code of Bauer's desire from her cross-dressed performance. In a poignant sex scene between Bauer and Clara, Clara lies naked on the bed and asks Bauer to also remove her clothes because it is "not fair" unless they are both naked and, by implication, vulnerable. Bauer slowly removes her clothes in front of a mirror. The camera focuses upon the mirror as if to suggest that, in the act of disrobing, Bauer's identity splinters and can no longer reflect her sexual desire. Clara coaxes Bauer to continue until Bauer sits in front of the mirror in an undershirt; not vulnerable now, but totally lost in the image that confronts her in the mirror. As Clara tries to touch her breasts, Bauer panics, grabs her clothes, and runs from the room.

In a review of *Vera* in 1987 in the *Village Voice,* B. Ruby Rich described this bedroom scene as evidence that Bauer has rejected lesbianism for "transsexual aspiration." Rich writes:

> *Vera* is a tough film to read. As a lesbian tale, it's problematic. Sure we know about the stone butches of the 50s, the girls who wouldn't let their femme lovers touch them, wouldn't take off their clothes in bed...but they knew they were dykes. Vera doesn't have a clue.[16]

This film is indeed "tough to read," but it is not exactly a case of Vera Bauer misreading her own lesbian desire. Bauer needs another woman to validate her gender fiction so that she can be the man she needs to be. Bauer must fuck in her clothes because her clothes represent her gender in a way that her anatomy cannot; but as long as anatomy is not destiny and as long as gender can perform a sexuality which appears to be at odds with biological sex, there is no reason that Bauer should undress. Indeed, the very act of dressing for Bauer is making herself vulnerable; she has bared her desire, she has revealed her sexuality and she makes explicit the gender performance that produces and is produced by her costume.

Bauer may not know she is a dyke, but she knows that she is not a woman. In a series of flashbacks to scenes from Bauer's childhood in the girls' reformatory, Toledo establishes a homosocial tension between the girls who divide up into butches and femmes. The director of the institution lines the butches up one day and warns, "I'm concerned about this butch-girl business." He looks them all up and down and then yells at them, "okay, you're so butch, let's see your pricks." Of course, butch does not require penile proof, a fleshly monument to "real" masculinity. Butch is a belief, a performance, a swagger in the walk; butch is an attitude, a tough line, a fiction, a way of dressing. But Bauer has no support for her butch performance: she is surrounded by people who must see her dick if they are to approve her masculinity, or her breasts if they are to prove her masculinity is simply a facade.

Clothes maketh the man and clothes make Bauer into a perfect icon of masculinity. Freud suggests that women cannot have fetishes since the fetish is what allows the little boy to sustain his belief in the mother's penis.[17] Bauer's cross-dressing sexuality, however, makes her a fetishist in that she is simultaneously the boy who refuses to acknowledge castration and the mother who both is and is not phallic. Clara refuses Bauer her act of fetishism. If Vera is a tragedy, then, it is a tragedy of misreading, not of gender dysphoria. Bauer needs a reader, needs an other to reflect her masculinity back to her in the form of desire. Without it she is reduced to the seemingly debased status of "stone butch," a kind of castrated lesbian, for all intents and purposes. But the "stone" in "stone butch" does not have to be a problem of inversion that requires surgery; as I have suggested throughout, masculinity or femininity *may* be simulated by surgery, but they can also find other fictional forms like clothing or fantasy. Bodily surgery is only one of many possibilities for remaking the gendered body.

*Vera* concludes with an ambiguous scene which marks

the dangers of gender rigidity. Bauer, rejected by her co-workers, her girlfriend, and now her foster family, sits crouched on a toilet and draws her hand out from between her legs, there is blood on it. It is not clear whether Bauer has mutilated herself or whether she is menstruating, and the two possibilities lead the film in very different directions. If Bauer has mutilated her genitals, then the closing shots of the body huddled in the bathroom mark the film as tragedy—the conclusion to gender dysphoria, in other words, is a lonely attack upon the immutability of the flesh itself. If the blood is menstrual blood, however, then the film concludes by confronting Bauer with her biology and allows an essentialist symbolism to creep into the picture. Either way, of course, the body loses and the conventions of gender win.

Bauer's masculinity, her desire to be a man who has sex with women, is no more or less precise or fixated than that of a genetic man who desires women, or a genetic woman who wants to be with a f-to-m, or a lesbian who wants to be naked with another lesbian, or a genetic female who wants to be a gay man having sex with two other genetic men, etc., etc. The term "stone butch" itself suggests that even (or especially) among lesbians there has been historically some inflexibility about the genders that we have authorized. Lesbians are also gendered, and the virtual explosion of information about and depictions of sexuality in recent times in lesbian sex magazines and zines attests to the ways in which what we have known as "lesbian sex" (sex between two genetic females being women) may be a marginal practice among many other sexual practices in the lesbian community. Discussions of butch-femme and s/m over the years have indicated that lesbians are also turned on by gendered sexual practices and restricted by the limiting of gender to bio-binarism.

We are all transgenders, I wrote earlier in this essay, and there are no transgenders. I want both claims to stand and find a place in relation to the postmodern lesbian body, the body dressed up in its gender or surgically constructed in the image of its gender. What is the relationship between the transsexual body, the transgendered body and the postmodern lesbian body? All threaten the binarism of homo/hetero sexuality by performing and fictionalizing gender. The postmodern lesbian body is a body fragmented by representation and theory, overexposed and yet inarticulate, finding a voice finally in the underground culture of zines and sex clubs.

Creating gender as fiction demands that we learn how to read it. In order to find our way into a post-transsexual era, we must educate ourselves as readers of gender-fiction, we must learn how to take pleasure in gender and how to become an audience for the multiple performances of gender that we witness every day. In a "Posttranssexual Manifesto" titled "The Empire Strikes Back," Sandy Stone also emphasizes the fictionality or readability of gender. She proposes that we constitute transsexuals as a "genre— a set of embodied texts whose potential for *productive* disruption of structured sexualities and spectra of desire has yet to be explored."[18] The "post" in "post-transsexual" demands, however, that we examine the strangeness of all gendered bodies, not only the trans-sexualized body, and that we rewrite the cultural fiction that divides a sex from a trans-sex, a gender from a transgender. All gender should be transgender; all desire is transgendered; movement is all.

The reinvention of lesbian sex, indeed of sex in general,

is an ongoing project and it coincides, as I have tried to show, with the formation of, or surfacing of, many other sexualities. The transgender community, for example, people in various stages of gender transition, have perhaps revealed the extent to which lesbians and gay men are merely the tip of the iceberg when it comes to identifying sexualities that defy heterosexual definition or the label "straight." The breakdown of genders and sexualities into identities is in many ways, therefore, an endless project and it is perhaps preferable therefore to acknowledge that gender is defined by its transitivity, that sexuality manifests as multiple sexualities and that therefore we are all transgenders. There are no transgenders.

## Notes

1. See Alice Echols, "The New Feminism of Yin Yang," in *Powers of Desire: The Politics of Sexuality,* ed. Ann Snitow, Christine Stansell and Sharon Thompson (New York: Monthly Review Press, 1983) pp. 439–459; and "The Taming of the Id: Feminist Sexual Politics, 1968-1983" in *Pleasure and Danger: Exploring Female Sexuality,* ed. Carole Vance (Boston and London: Routledge, Kegan Paul, 1984) pp. 50–72.

2. Interview, "Guys with Pussies" by Chris Martin with "Vern and Danny." Part of this interview was published in *Movement Research Performance Journal* #3 (Fall 1991) pp. 6–7.

3. Interview with Chris Martin, "World's Greatest Cocksucker," in *Movement Research Journal* #3 (Fall 1991) p. 6.

4. See for example Marcie Sheiner, "Some Girls Will Be Boys," in *On Our Backs* (March/April 1991) p. 20.

5. Alisa Solomon, "Drag Race: Rites of Passing," *The Village Voice* (November 15, 1991) p. 46.

6. For example see Kaja Silverman, *Masculinity in the Margins* (New York: Routledge, 1992) or Victor Seidler, *Rediscovering Masculinity: Reason, Language and Sexuality* (London and New York: Routledge, 1989).

7. Marjorie Garber, *Vested Interests: Cross-Dressing and Cultural Anxiety* (New York: Routledge, 1992) p. 16.

8. Ibid, 109.

9. Jan Morris, *Conundrum* (New York: Harcourt, Brace, Jovanovich, 1974).

10. As I was writing this piece, I read in a copy of *Seattle Gay News* (January 1992) that a transsexual group in Seattle were meeting to discuss how to maintain the definition of transsexual operations as medical rather than cosmetic, because if they are termed "cosmetic" then insurance companies can refuse to pay for them. As always, discursive effects are altered by capitalist relations in ways that are unforeseeable. I do not think we should give up on the cosmeticization of transsexualism in order to appease insurance companies: rather we should argue that cosmetics are never separate from

"health" and insurance companies should not be the ones making such distinctions, anyway.

11. Robert Scheer, "The Cosmetic Surgery Revolution: Risks and Rewards," *Los Angeles Times* (December 22, 1991) A1, A24, A42.

12. Garber, *Vested Interests*, p. 117.

13. Bornstein's play, *The Opposite Sex is Neither* played in San Diego at the Sushi Performance Gallery, December 13-14, 1991. The quotation is from "Transsexual Lesbian Playwright Tells All" in *High Risk,* ed. Amy Scholder and Ira Silverberg (New York: Penguin, 1991) p. 261.

14. Judith Butler, *Gender Trouble: Feminism and the Subversion of Identity* (New York: Routledge, 1990) p. 123. The sentence reads: "As one lesbian femme explained, she likes her boys to be girls, meaning that 'being a girl' contextualizes and resignifies 'masculinity' in a butch identity."

15. Cathy Opie, *Scream Box* #1 (November, 1990) p.11.

16. B. Ruby Rich, "Vera," *The Village Voice* (October 20, 1987).

17. See Sigmund Freud, "Fetishism" (1927) in *Sexuality and the Psychology of Love,* ed. Philip Rieff (New York: Collier, 1963) p. 214–219.

18. Sandy Stone, "The *Empire* Strikes Back: A Posttranssexual Manifesto" in *Body Guards: The Cultural Politics of Gender Ambiguity,* ed. Julia Epstein and Kristina Straub (New York: Routledge, 1991) p. 296.

## EILEEN MYLES
## Campaign Diaries

### I. Dear Madonna, June 9, 1991

I'm confused. Why are you going to such lengths to convince the world you are not a lesbian? We don't care if you're one or not, but why does it worry you so? I like the photographs in the June *Rolling Stone* of you kissing girls and you also look great in drag. In your interview with (barf!) Carrie Fisher you stated: "Oh I believe in everything." That's a great and inclusive public stance. It definitely suits your pro-art anti-censorship presence in the media which so many of us truly admire. And you're publicly pro-gay, which we also love. Last night I saw your new film *Truth or Dare,* and in it were included clips from a Queer Nation March. But where were the girls? What is this funny business you're dishing out about lesbians? But, back to the interview. After Carrie Fisher brilliantly states: "There's no way to look at someone who has strapped on a dildo and still think they're human. Their dignity levels are frighteningly low," you, Madonna, reply that you "had a friend strap one on and you couldn't stop laughing..." you continued, "so I can't see how anyone could look at them with a straight face." Madonna, you are missing the point entirely. You state in the same interview that when you as a little girl saw your first penis you "thought they were disgusting." Something similar happens around dildos. I'm a lesbian and I have used dildos and of course they're funny-looking. It's not "serious." They are a joke that works. Women who are really into dildos come to love the way they look. It's exaggerated, super-transgressive and, because many lesbians would love to fuck another woman with a dick, it's a fantasy! One I also recall you sharing in this same interview. Of course if you don't love dildos you can use your fingers (remember that girl in junior high, Madonna) or a whole hand or some girls even like a fist. It's smaller than a baby's head, they say. I guess I think it was brave of you to say in *Rolling Stone* that you've had fantasies of fucking women, and I quote: "Yeah, I'd like to know what it feels like to go in and out of somebody" but if you've never been fucked by one (unless you've forgotten that, too) how do you know you're not a lesbian? Your certainty is the note in this interview that I thought was anti-sex. I'm pro-queer, you proclaim, but I'm not one! Not me, uh-uh, no way! It takes all the panache out of your cross-dressing if you need to set us straight—assuring us (and who is us, Madonna? At the moment, it's me.) It's just a tease. Teasing don't work that way. And what about a man in a dress, Carrie Fisher? How about if he puts on a pair of tits? Is he less than human? Are his dignity levels frighteningly low? Or is it just female homosexuality—try femaleness—that's once again frightening, the thing we hate? Especially in a ludicrous and aggressive pose—a girl who would strap on a dick— disgusting! Try it Madonna, Truth or Dare.

Sincerely,
Eileen Myles

## II. Pixel Speaks

I've been scratching and fussing for days about how to give a real living breathing portrait of the emotional reality of being a lesbian star. A lesbian film star and you know my moment is really already past so it's a tragic piece of journalism I'm about at the moment. I had the distinction of being in four, yeah four count 'em, vehicles in the New (Lesbian and Gay) Film Festival at the Quad. The first thing, and probably the only thing I can tell you about how you can get in on this action for yourself is you have to be intimately involved with a lesbian film- or videomaker. Which is very convenient for everyone. Otherwise if someone asks you to be in their film or video, you are better off being a little on the naïve side. It'll just take a few hours. Maybe next winter I'll come in town to shoot, would that be possible? And you say, sure sure. Looking back on my approximately—oh, less than an hour of screen exposure—l realize I was in four videos, not films so I'm more of a pixel than a star. I'm sure you know what a pixel is, right. I mean a star flickers, is up there in the deep brooding black of the night. But a pixel is just like a dumb little American voter, one of millions of various teeny cubes that make up the picture that is being manipulated. At least half of the videos that I was in were shot in my apartment, and it occurs to me that my dog was in two out of the four vehicles and one of them was a campaign documentary (*Poet in the Ring*) shot by my lover (Jennifer Montgomery) so you get the idea that there was no platonic art making going on, but a very colloquial spread was being assembled, I didn't have to clean, I could sit on the toilet, make phone calls in one case (*Poet in the Ring*) and otherwise hang out with a number of people I might normally be hanging out with in my apartment as long as I basically said word for word what Leslie ("Taking Back the Dolls") Singer had sent me in the mail that week. So it was regular, but it was manipulated. Then she sent me a dub of what she shot and I sent her a postcard back telling her what I thought. I watched it at home on my own teevee so I suppose the biggest shock for this pixel was sitting in the Quad looking at a much bigger version of that stuff and I could not pause, rewind. Julie Zando's shoot (*Uh Oh*), both the summer and the winter experiences, was the most exotic. I sat around someone's apartment in Tivoli, New York, one afternoon in a maroon bathrobe smoking cigarette after cigarette occasionally having fierce make-out scenes with Emanuela, who played "Oh." I guess I was "Uh." I was pretty confused that summer about whether I should have tagged along with Jennifer to Bard—but at least during the week of Julie's shoot I had this instant community and we walked around in long flowing gowns wearing big dildos. Mostly I was embarrassed that I couldn't just throw myself into simulated sex with twelve people watching. I was better at the small, private, make-out scenes. Though what they reminded me of was junior high when we were practicing on other girls, and not necessarily the ones we wanted, in order to learn how to make out with boys. You just had this abnormal sense of the other person's smell and surface, in both experiences, because you had elected to be there for some reason other than your true sex drive. Also I was not drunk. But, rather, stone sober and *pretending* to be passionately making out. You don't expect that to be happening twice in your life. Because I am not an actor. Was that okay, I'd ask earnestly. Don't worry, I'm sure I got something. I'm thinking I looked like a real stud, while whoever was shooting may well have been getting my feet. 'Cause that's what they thought was really interesting. It's not a human thing, film. I mean, video.

It's June 1994. As always, I think about my dog. Around twilight she was cavorting in a playground on East Fourth Street. I was relaxing on a bench, wishing I could stay there forever. All summer, on that bench, this exact light, not going away for the perfect summer somewhere, not trying to have it. Here, utterly here. Like Rosie, unflawed. I'm jealous of my dog. Who is really a star. I was busily blowing another star opportunity. I had donated a kit of campaign kitsch to Astraea for their auction and probably my contribution was on the block right now. I had had a busy day and just kind of swooned when it was time to pedal over to Soho and be cool. Part of my kit were thirty-two different buttons, black-and-white and color Xeroxes, more pixels, which documented a summer night much like this in 1991, when Jennifer took pictures of a much younger Rosie & that night, now lodged on inexpensive buttons coated in plastic which were at this moment being valued at the Drawing Center and would someone pay fifty bucks or a hundred or three hundred and fifty for the thirty-two round little depictions of a night irretrievably lost (and even a presidential campaign) and this one going down the drain as we speak, growing darker; but Rosie was having none of these thoughts, not that night or this one, but gleaming irreverently and eternally with her tongue hanging out panting, lying in the sand and it was really cool (the sand) and it was the happiest part of her day, and I loved her so completely in a way the movies make so invisible. She was truly a star, irretrievably so in her forgetful moment of bliss. And I am absolutely not. I am a pixel, and then maybe a poet.

When I watch me on the screen in a room full of hundreds of girls (*Lesbian Avengers Eat Fire*) I'm obsessed with everything that can't be seen, the secrets of that long-gone day. Then I go to the closing of the New (Lesbian & Gay) Festival and I described it later on the phone. How the microphone was handed from man to man (mispronouncing several women's names along the way) and so was the check for the new award. The meaning's at the end as everyone knows. They're the separatists, not us, said Leslie.

### Campaign Diary: April 7, 1992

Primary day in New York and I'm flying to Buffalo, having had the exquisite pleasure of going into the curtained election booth, pulling down the red lever while holding the small silver button with a finger of my left hand and then panicking because I had left my black pen on the floor and I couldn't let go of that button so I howled until the guy who showed me how to do it unsurely leaned in and picked it up for me. Also there's also a small slide you move as well and there it sits, the blank space under President and I write it in, my name; and you may think it's crazy, but it really feels great.

The streets were wider when I walked home and I found myself thinking I've done it all wrong, waging a write-in campaign and maybe it might've been better for everyone in America who feels the election process is a joke to write in their own names, so they might feel great too. My finger hurts. I smashed it in East River Head Park when I was trying to get my pit, Rosie, on her leash. First she grabbed a little tiny football away from a kid and his father who were throwing it back and forth. Then she grabbed a big softball from a boy and a girl who were tossing it around. That was troublesome. I warned them, but the ball dropped and the kid, disbelieving, watched as Rosie got it. And I couldn't get it back for anything.

I grabbed what appeared to be one of the big rubber witch's hats you see on the highway, orange ones, for construction. I figured they were building something here. Well, they weren't. It was being used as a marker for sprinters who were whirling happily around the track until I wrecked their game. She shouldn't be off her leash, barked their leader. It was close to six, the sun was setting, it was getting cold, and Rosie was still gleefully prancing around with the kid's ball. I kept throwing sticks at her, trying anything to distract her from their toy, but mostly it appeared I was attacking her with a barrage of available satellites, and I was. I was pissed and I was late. Somewhere in there I socked my middle finger with a witch's hat, I threw it at her (which is how I got the little football away) and she butted it back joyfully, smarter now, on to my game and I felt a twinge in my finger and knew something was coming and it has. I've had a dark purple finger for most of a week.

That night I rushed to the WAC meeting, a women's

action group which meets in Soho and addressed them briefly, maniacally, and into a cab to the Ninth Street Theater. They were having a dinner, and I was the after-dinner speaker. The top of the show. I told them how it feels to be female, the little superior game room at the Catholic Youth Center was not available to me, nor was any of the entire Arlington Boys Center which sat big and blue in front of Spy Pond, reminding me and all girls in my town that we weren't good enough. And now out wheatpasting (eight reasons why you should write in Eileen Myles for President in '92) in midtown—at the Helmsley walkway with a black chador-like scarf covering my face. Jennifer in a hood, ducking the cameras, then a voice—"Get out of here, you little shits!" and we ran. Took a train downtown and practically sat on the grime of ancient cities on the platform at Grand Central—the baby is back! Next night—oh, we were coming back from D.C. I saw Bill Clinton's entourage. "Hey, Bill"—and I tapped his back and thrust my position paper on choice at him. "This might help you." He does need a lot of help, that guy. We stumbled into the Nancy Hanks Center, home of the NEA which has denied me so much money over the years, and now it was endless yogurt stands and international food and thousands of marchers sipping cappuccino.

After eating, a moment on the grass near the speakers' stand and on to the subway, not nervously yet, to the Pentagon. Still leafleting—"Pro-Choice Candidate!" NOBODY KNOWS I'M ME is the secret slogan of my campaign. Having no face recognition, I can do all the work for me I want, and nobody will know. Nobody knows the other candidates either, Karen points out. Come Monday...we were leafleting. Jennifer had Peggy's camera—we went uptown.

I leafleted cabs, trucks, we went in to MOMA and campaigned to a row of beautiful giggling Corsicans and two pro-life girls all pinky and angry. It was a great day. Karen and I went up to Different Light. At night—the night when candidates pray—I had dinner with David, Jennifer, and Lin. We had curry. We had no napkins and I had to run down to the store. You'd think it was the end of the world when I got the call that said I'd been rejected for a very posh grant. It's okay, I already knew. I then sank so low. Have I forgotten I'm running for president? To be elected one must put her head, her life on the chopping block, make all kinds of fools of herself because it is the biggest show of all in America and I just wanted to say, a woman, me, I could come.

I've been running for president for a year now. I've watched candidates come and go in the tabloids (Cuomo Won't, or Will He? Stuff like that) and it seems to me that a small campaign is the way to be consistent. Maybe the media attention diverts a candidate from her own best intentions. I experienced an onslaught of diversion just last week on a stoop on East Third Street where I live. MTV News was coming to pay a call. Allison Stewart had heard me at Dixon Place. She said they were interested in bringing out the 18–24-year-old vote, thus me (I'm 42, but so what, huh?). I did some preparatory thinking about parental consent which seemed like a serious youth issue. Re abortion and HIV-testing. Originally we planned to conduct the interview at Mogador, but they balked I was told. So we used my neighbor's stoop and reality began. I watch a thin young MTV man cross the street and ask the Hell's Angels to turn their music down. Oldies blare twenty-four hours a day. The Hell's Angel stood in place as if he hadn't felt a breeze, never mind the young man's request. The Angel just stood there. I walked across and pointed out I have lived here for years and they are MTV and it would be just a few minutes.

During all of this (and earlier when I was walking up the street with them and their cameras) neighbors were asking, "What's this all about?"

"I'm running for president," I told the woman stepping out of the spiritualist storefront.

"President of what?"

"President of the United States of America," I replied, and she shook with silent laughter. You are nuts, she blared silently. I'm getting used to this. I go into galleries to look at the art, and the director goes "How's the campaign?" and gives me a big silent horselaugh.

So I sit down on the steps with Tabitha, the MTV interviewer who informs me she's sick so if she seems a little out of it…. The Angels have turned the music down a bit, though assuring me there are reasons why it's on. Yeah, you like the past, and you like it loud. Everybody from MTV (who are young, in their 20s) likes the looks of my neighborhood, but not the sounds of it. We are intruding. I know that. It's not my stoop, so when Nunie, a fat little Hispanic kid, runs up his steps and buzzes his buzzer and winds up having a loud conversation with his mother over the intercom, Tabitha and MTV look really bugged. I'm bugged, too. Hey, Nunie, can't you give us a few minutes? I keep trying to talk about parental consent, but I really feel a wall. I try to explain and Tabitha goes yeah, yeah. I talk about the obvious things: I'm female, I'm gay, I am not rich, etc., how I represent people like myself I even try and talk about the media but somehow the whole thing feels like a washout. I know my dog looks great.

Two days later I'm in the Washington Square dog run. "Hey, was that dog on MTV?" a guy asks. "You look familiar, too. Are you running for president or something? No, it wasn't clear why you were running," he says. "But you got a lot of airtime. Joe Westmoreland, my campaign secretary, tapes it next time it airs.

I don't even have cable, but they're coming today to install it. The morning before I go out of town, I watch the clip. I look sort of old. I explain the mechanics of the write-in ballot ("Pull the lever, push the button, slide the silver thing, and a white space appears, and there you write in your own name. It feels great!"). Then all the other candidates come on: Fulani, Agren, a libertarian, and Perot. Then Myles again: "So a vote for me is a vote for you." But why?

A few days later I'm in riot-torn L.A. The most interesting story is that a Beverly Hills jewelry store did a looting-oriented window just two days after the riots. With bricks and flames and jewelry around the necks of the mannequins. My culture astonishes me. We're watching *Saturday Night Live* in our hotel room, and it seems obscene and racist. I call my machine. The phone rings and rings. I guess I was cleaned out, I joke. I call a few friends with keys to my place to turn on my machine, but nothing changes as I continue to call. When I get in on Sunday night, there's my VCR in a bag pulled out of my closet. There's my gate pulled out of my wall. This hasn't happened in years. Thanks to the Angels I live on a safe block. (As long as you're white. As long as I don't kiss my girlfriend in the street. That ticks the Angels' girlfriends off—"You know I've got a kid here, you lezzy bitch.") Years ago I played very loud music and my sensitive neighbor Carl always complained. "Can't you turn it down, Eileen?" Yet Carl's good ears heard someone on the fire escape and called the cops. They nabbed him in here and now he's in jail. My super tells me they're still looking for his tools. How did he open the window? Well that black bag on my bed isn't mine. Here's his little red flashlight, here's his screwdriver, here's a big metal crowbar, here's a pencil, a gray pad of legal paper and a giveaway magazine. I've been calling friends for the past couple of days. Listen, if we're broke this summer, I've got a business we can start. Nobody wants to get involved but they're putting their orders in. If you see a stereo, or just a CD player. Once again I'm on my own. Per the D.A.'s request, I drop the bag off at the Ninth Precinct, and as usual, my dog's a smash. Two women come in for restraining orders just while I'm sitting there in a little blue chair. On 3/2/92 Phil Jackson, a skinny white junkie broke into my apartment. He put my VCR into my orange bicycle bag. If he sold it on the street, it would contain an excerpt of me on MTV running for president. A vote for me is a vote for you. Some not-so-silent laughter. It's been one hell of a campaign.

### Campaign Diary, May 23, 1992

Mr. Quayle says that a welfare check is not a father and the government is not a father. We know that. Does anyone anywhere look at a check they received in the mail & go Hello, Daddy?

What I want to talk about this evening is sperm. 'Cause if the government or the government's money is not a father, then sperm is probably not a father either, though both of them sit in a bank. Money is power and so is sperm, and I have recently noticed that some men are threatened to the point of violence when women seek to gain control of either one of them. I'm referring of course to two recent encounters with sperm and those concern rape and what do you call it—artificial insemination. (Whose dick? Nobody's! Sounds fake to me). Let's do rape first. We all remember of course the case of the fourteen-year-old Irish girl who was raped at a pajama party by her friend's father. She and her family actually hightailed it to London to get the abortion, but once there contacted the Irish government because they were concerned that aborting the fetus might destroy evidence that could be used against the rapist, and that triggered the whole thing we all know about. The Irish government would not allow the girl to leave, and that is the international incident that is so well known.

In March I was in Cleveland to do a performance and to publicize the festival I was being a part of. I was invited to be on a radio talk show with a guy named Merle—I think that was his name. It was great. I took a cab to that part of town and arrived at the station that was at a mall or something—an arcade. I went briefly into an office, and then I was ushered into the Plexiglas-and-gold studio that overlooks makeup counters and patisseries and newsstands. Nothing special, but very plastic and bright. And there I sat at this table with tons of plugs in front of me, and I wore headphones and I faced Merle. There's certain machines at the gym where I go where you wind up facing someone who's doing the other half of the machine. It's some kind of modern pillory. Kind of like fucking. It was like that with Merle, his big face, a Polish uncle from Cleveland. Why am I telling you this? He was not unfamiliar. Quite the opposite, in fact. Anyway, the reason I was really on was that I am running for president of the United States. I am a lesbian presidential candidate, and that's why I was on Merle's show. In fact, it quickly became clear that he just wanted to talk to me about being a dyke. Why am I telling you this? Because it was utterly clear when I talked to Merle that the crux of all his problems with homosexuals was that we seem to think that we deserved the same things as he did. Had "rights." But in fact this was his country. He owned it, and why did we think he should give us this or this or this? My task on his show was to continually remind him that I lived here. That I was an American, that I paid taxes. Was a citizen. All his prejudices towards me came out of a supposition that I was an alien, an outsider to his culture and I was moving in a hostile manner and making demands. Every time he came at me with this stuff, there was this same gaping hole in his logic.

Why am I telling you this? During a commercial, we had a little talk. We were off the air. He said, "You know, my niece is a lesbian. So I'm not far away from all this as it might seem. You know, I'm on my show. I've got to play around with you a little bit. Anyhow, the reason I mention this is that my niece—she's a psychiatrist, very smart girl like yourself—and her girlfriend decided to do the artificial insemination, and the whole family ignored it when the child was born. I didn't. I bought them a present. I thought what the hell, I had to do that. It's human. But you know just between you and me I think it's wrong. That's what I really have a problem with. Two women going to the bank and buying the stuff. It's just not right—Whoops! Gotta go back on the air."

Now, this is what fascinates me. There's some correlation here. Between the Irish government trying to force a fourteen-year-old girl in front of the eyes of the world to give birth to a child born out of rape in a friend's house and a man privately telling me off the air that there's nothing wrong with lesbianism—very many of us are nice girls— but there is something very wrong with one woman spurting a little bit of sperm between her lover's legs into her body to bear a child that will be nurtured by their relationship. At the bottom of both of these situations is a deep-seated male horror of female control of the traffic of sperm. Or, in the case of Mr. Quayle, a horror of male absence. If a man— any man—has planted sperm in a female's body, that is okay. She may not remove it. And she may not direct it. She may not contain it, freeze it, carry it, shoot it, own its products. The dictionary defines sperm as the originative matter from which something develops. The female is not part of this definition. "She" is the outsider to the birth process. It's the law. Why am I telling you this?

I was reading in the *Times* about the environmental conference in Rio de Janeiro. As you probably know, the developing nations (those having resources) came up with some guidelines to protect what they have where they live, and the developed countries opposed them, wouldn't sign. Developed means you make things, are industrial, or, truer, make investments in developing nations. Like where you plant your sperm. When Mr. Quayle shakes his fist at Candice Bergen, it's because she's a Third World country that has its own show. She took the money and ran.

Now what about Ross Perot. Such a big outsider. World's richest woman, obviously. Who's buying America on his birthday this year. Stay tuned on June 27. He's banning you from a cabinet post if you're queer. Who says queers in the military are inappropriate? Why? We're a security risk. Why? Because we can be blackmailed. Because of homophobia. What *is* homophobia? When Bill Clinton says, "I'm not sure I'm prepared to say I would support that," in reference to domestic-partnership laws, and a gay magazine that just changed its name endorses his campaign, I'd say that's homophobia. Many Americans like Ross Perot because he speaks his mind. And Hitler never called Jews outsiders, he just claimed that they were an infection. Like HIV? Put your money where your mouth is. WRITE ME IN.

PART TWO:

# Personal Reflections

## DOROTHY ALLISON
# from Believing in Literature

I have always passionately loved good books—good stories and beautiful writing and, most of all, books that seemed to me to be intrinsically important, books that told the truth, painful truths sometimes, in a voice that made eloquent the need for human justice. That is what I have meant when I have used the word "literature." It has seemed to me that literature, as I meant it, was embattled, that it was increasingly difficult to find writing doing what I thought literature should do—which was simply to push people into changing their ideas about the world, and to go further, to encourage us in the work of changing the world, to making it more just and more truly human.

All my life I have hated clichés, the clichés applied to people like me and those I love. Every time I pick up a book that purports to be about either poor people or queers or Southern women, I do so with a conscious anxiety, an awareness that the books about us have often been cruel, small, and false. I have wanted our lives taken seriously and represented fully—with power and honesty and sympathy—to be hated or loved, or to terrify and obsess, but to be real, to have the power of the whole and the complex. I have never wanted politically correct parables made out of my grief, simpleminded rote speeches made from my rage, simplifications that reduce me to cardboard dimensions. But mostly that is what I have found. We are the ones they make fiction of—we queer and disenfranchised and female—and we have the right to demand our full, nasty, complicated lives, if only to justify all the times our reality has been stolen, mismade, and dishonored.

That our true stories may be violent, distasteful, painful, stunning, and haunting, I do not doubt. But our true stories will be literature. No one will be able to forget them; and though it will not always make us happy to read of the dark and dangerous places in our lives, the impact of our reality is the best we can ask of our literature.

Literature, and my own dream of writing, has shaped my system of belief—a kind of atheist's religion. I gave up God and the church early on, choosing instead to place all my hopes in direct-action politics. But the backbone of my convictions has been a belief in the progress of human society as demonstrated in its fiction. Even as a girl I believed that our writing was better than we were. There were, after all, those many novels of good and evil, of working-class children shown to be valuable and sympathetic human beings, of social criticism and subtle education—books that insisted we could be better than we were. I used my belief in the power of good writing as a way of giving meaning to some of the injustices I saw around me.

When I was very young, still in high school, I thought about writing the way Fay Weldon outlined in her essay, "The City of Imagination," in *Letters to My Niece on First Reading Jane Austen.* I imagined that Literature was, as she named it, a city with many districts, or was like a great library of the human mind that included all the books ever written. But what was most important was the enormous diversity contained in that library of the mind, that imaginary city. I cruised that city and dreamed of being part of it, but I was fearful that anything I wrote would be relegated to unimportance—no matter how finely crafted my writing might be, no matter how hard I worked and how much I risked. I knew I was a lesbian, and I believed that meant I would always be a stranger in the city—unless I performed the self-defeating trick of disguising my imagination, hiding my class origin and sexual orientation, writing, perhaps, a comic novel about the poor or the sexually dysfunctional. If that was the only way in, it made sense to me how many of the writers I loved drank or did drugs or went slowly crazy, trying to appear to be something they were not. It was enough to convince me that there was no use in writing at all.

When feminism exploded in my life, it gave me a vision of the world totally different from everything I had ever assumed or hoped. The concept of a feminist literature offered the possibility of pride in my sexuality. It saved me from either giving up writing entirely, or the worse prospect of writing lies in order to achieve some measure of grudging acceptance. But at the same time, Feminism destroyed all my illusions about Literature. Feminism revealed the city as an armed compound to which I would never be admitted. It forced me to understand, suddenly and completely, that literature was written by men, judged by men. The city itself was a city of Man, a male mind even when housed in a female body. If that was so, all my assumptions about the worth of writing, particularly working-class writing, were false. Literature was a lie, a system of lies, the creation of liars, some of them sincere and unaware of the lies they retold, but all acting in the service of a Great Lie—what the system itself labeled Universal Truth. If that truth erased me and all those like me, then my hopes to change the world through writing were illusions. I lost my faith. I became a feminist activist propelled in part by outrage and despair, and a stubborn determination to shape a life, and create a literature, that was not a lie.

I think many lesbian and feminist writers my age had a similar experience. The realizations of feminist criticism made me feel as if the very ground on which I stood had become unsteady. Some of that shakeup was welcome and hopeful, but it also meant that I had to make a kind of life raft for myself out of political conviction, which is why I desperately needed a feminist community and so feared being driven out of the one I found. I know many other women who felt the same way; who grew up in poverty and got their ideas of what might be possible from novels of social criticism, believing those books were about us even when they were obviously not. What the feminist critique of patriarchal literature meant was not only that all we had believed about the power of writing to change the world was not possible, but that to be true to our own vision, we had to create a new canon, a new literature. Believing in literature—a feminist literature—became a reason to spend my life in that pursuit.

There are times I have wondered if that loss of faith was really generational, or only my own. I have seen evidence of a similar attitude in the writing of many working-class lesbians who are my age peers, the sense of having been driven out of the garden of life, and a painful pride in that exile through still mourning the dream of worth and meaning. The feminist small-press movement was created out of that failed belief and the hope of reestablishing a literature that we could believe in. Daughters, Inc., Know, Inc., Diana Press, *Amazon Quarterly, Quest, Conditions*...right down to *OUT/ LOOK*. All those magazines and presses—the ones I have worked with and supported even when I found some of the writing tedious or embarrassing—were begun in that spirit of rejecting the false ideal for a true one. This was a very mixed enterprise at its core, because creating honest work in which we did not have to mask our actual experiences, or our sexuality and gender, was absolutely the right thing to do; but rejecting the established literary canon was not simple, and throwing out the patriarchy put so much else in question. Many of us lost all sense of what could be said to be good or bad writing, or how to think about being writers while bypassing the presses, grants, and teaching programs that might have helped us devote the majority of our time to writing, to creating a body of work.

The difficulty faced by lesbian and feminist writers of my generation becomes somewhat more understandable if we think about the fact that almost no lesbian-feminist writer my age was able to make a living as a writer. Most of us wrote late at night after exhausting and demanding day jobs, after evenings and weekends of political activism, meetings, and demonstrations. Most of us also devoted enormous amounts of time and energy to creating presses and journals that embodied our political ideals, giving up the time and energy we might have used to actually do our writing. During my involvement with *Quest,* I wrote one article. The rest of my writing time was given over to grant applications and fund-raising letters. I did a little better with *Conditions,* beginning to actually publish short stories, but the vast majority of work I did there was editing other people's writing and, again, writing grants and raising money. Imagine how few paintings or sculptures would be created if the artists all had to collectively organize the creation of canvas and paint, build and staff the galleries, and turn back all the money earned from sales into the maintenance of the system. Add to that the difficulty of creating completely new philosophies about what would be suitable subjects for art, what approaches would be valid for artists to take to their work, who, in fact, would be allowed to say what was valuable and what was not, or more tellingly, what could be sold and to whom. Imagine that system and you have the outlines of some of the difficulties faced by lesbian writers of my generation.

As a writer, I think I lost at least a decade in which I might have done more significant work because I had no independent sense of my work's worth. If Literature was a dishonest system by which the work of mediocre men and women could be praised for how it fit into a belief system that devalued women, queers, people of color, and the poor, then how could I try to become part of it? Worse, how could I judge any piece of writing, how could I know what was good or bad, worthwhile or a waste of time? To write for that system was to cooperate in your own destruction, certainly in your misrepresentation. I never imagined that what we were creating was also limited, that it, too, reflected an unrealistic or dishonest vision. But that's what we did, at least in part, making an ethical system that insists a lightweight romance has the same worth as a serious piece of fiction, that there is no good or bad, no "objective" craft or standards of excellence....

▲▼▲

Everything I know, everything I put in my fiction, will hurt someone somewhere as surely as it will comfort and enlighten someone else. What, then, is my responsibility? What am I to restrain? What am I to fear and alter—my own nakedness or the grief of the reader?

My students are invariably determined that their stories will be powerful, effective, crafted, and unforgettable, not the crap that so embarrasses them. "Uh-huh," I nod at them, not wanting to be patronizing but remembering when I was twenty-four and determined to start my own magazine, to change how people thought about women, poor people, lesbians, and literature itself. Maybe it will be different in their lifetimes, I think, though part of me does believe it is different already. But more is possible than has yet been accomplished, and what I have done with my students is plant a seed that I expect to blossom in a new generation.

Once in a while one of my students will ask me, "Why have there been no great lesbian novels?" I do not pretend that they are wrong, do not tell them how many of the great writers of history were lesbians. They and I know that a lesbian author does not necessarily write a lesbian novel. Most often I simply disagree and offer a list of what I believe to be good lesbian writing. It is remarkable to me that as soon as I describe some wonderful story being by a lesbian, there is always someone who wants to argue whether the individual involved really deserves that label. I no longer participate in this pointless argument. I feel that as a lesbian I have a perfect right to identify some writing as lesbian regardless of whether the academy or contemporary political theorists would agree with me. What I find much more interesting is that so many of my gay and lesbian and feminist students are unaware of their own community's history. They may have read *Common Lives / Lesbian Lives, On Our Backs,* or various 'zines, and joke about any magazine that could publish such trivial fiction, believing the magazines contemptible because they do not edit badly written polemics and true confessions. But few of them know anything about the ideology that made many of us in the 1970s abandon the existing literary criteria to create our own.

We believed that editing itself was a political act, and we questioned what was silenced when raw and rough work by women outside the accepted Literary canon was written or edited in such a way that the authentic voices were erased. My students have no sense of how important it was to let real women tell their stories in their own words. I try to explain, drawing their attention to ethnographies and oral histories, techniques that reveal what is so largely shown in traditionally edited fiction—powerful, unusual voices not recognized by the mainstream. I tell them how much could not be published or even written before the creation of the queer and lesbian presses which honored that politic. I bring in old copies of Daughters books: not *Rubyfruit Jungle,* which they know, but *The True Story of a Drunken Mother* by Nancy Hall, which mostly they haven't seen. I make it personal and tell them bluntly that I would never have begun to write anything of worth without the example of those presses and magazines reassuring me that my life, and my family's life, was a fit subject for literature.

As I drag my poor students through my own version of the history of lesbian and gay publishing, I am painfully aware that the arguments I make that I pretend are so clear and obvious—are still completely unresolved. I pretend to my students that there is no question about the value of writing, even though I know I have gone back and forth from believing totally in it to being convinced that books never really change anything and are only published if they don't offend people's dearly held prejudices too much. So, affecting confidence, I still worry about what I truly believe about literature and my writing.

Throughout my work with the lesbian and gay, feminist, and small-press movements, I went on reading the enemy—mainstream literature—with a sense of guilt and uncertainty that I might be in some way poisoning my mind, and wondering, worrying, trying to develop some sense of worth outside purely political judgments. I felt like an apostate who still mumbles prayers in moments of crisis. I wanted to hear again the equivalent of the still, small voice of God telling me: Yes, Dorothy, books are important. Fiction is a piece of truth that turns lies to meaning. Even outcasts can write great books. I wanted to be told that it is only the form that has failed, that the content was still there—like a Catholic who returns to God but never the church.

The result has been that after years of apostasy, I have come make distinctions between what I call the academy and literature, the moral equivalents of the church and God. The academy may lie, but literature tries to tell the truth.

The academy is the market—university courses in contemporary literature that never get past Faulkner, reviewers who pepper their opinions with the ideas of the great men, and editors who think something is good because it says the same thing everyone has always said. Literature is the lie that tells the truth, that shows us human beings in pain and makes us love them, and does so in a spirit of honest revelation. That's radical enough, and more effective than only publishing unedited oral history. It is the stance I assumed when I decided I could not live without writing fiction and trying to publish it for the widest possible audience. It is the stance I maintain as I try to make a living by writing, supplemented with teaching, and to publish with both a mainstream publishing house and a small lesbian press. What has been extraordinarily educational and difficult to accept these past few years of doing both has been the recognition that the distinction between the two processes is nowhere near as simple or as easily categorized as I had once thought.

In 1989, when I made the decision to take my novel *Bastard Out of Carolina* to a mainstream press, I did so in part because I did not believe I could finish it without financial help. I was broke, sick, and exhausted. My vision had become so bad that I could no longer assume I could go back at any time to doing computer work or part-time clerical jobs. I had to either find a completely new way to make a living and devote myself to that enterprise, or accept the fact that I was going to have to try to get an advance that would buy me at least two years to finish the book. Finally, I also knew that this book had become so important to me that I *had* to finish it, even if it meant doing something I had never assumed I would do. Reluctantly, I told Nancy Bereano what I was doing with *Bastard,* and then approached a friend to ask him to act as my agent. I had never worked with an agent before, but all my political convictions convinced me I could not trust mainstream presses and did not know enough to be able to deal with them. In fact, I learned while doing journalism in New York in the 1980s, that I was terrible at the business end of writing, rotten at understanding the arcane language of contracts. In some ways my worst fears were realized. Selling a manuscript to strangers is scary.

What most surprised me, however, was learning that mainstream publishing was not a monolith, and finding there not only people who believed in literature the way I did, but lesbians and gay men who worked within mainstream publishing because of their belief in the importance of good writing and how it can change the world. Mostly younger, and without my experience of the lesbian and gay small presses, they talked in much the same way as I did about their own convictions, the jobs they took that demanded long hours and paid very poorly but let them work, at least in part, with writing and writers whom they felt vindicated their sacrifices. Talking to those men and women shook up a lot of my assumptions, particularly when I began to work with heterosexuals who did not seem uniformly homophobic or deluded or crassly obsessed with getting rich as quickly as possible. I found within mainstream publishing a great many sincere and hopeful people of conviction and high standards who forced me to reexamine some of my most ingrained prejudices. If I was going to continue to reject the ideology and standards of mainstream literature, I had to become a lot more clear and specific about the distinction between the patriarchal literature I had been trying to challenge all my life and the good-hearted individuals I encountered within those institutions.

As I was finishing the copyediting of *Bastard,* I found myself thinking about all I had read when Kate Millett published *Flying:* her stated conviction that telling the truth was what feminist writers were supposed to do. That telling the truth—your side of it anyway, knowing that there were truths other than your own—was a moral act, a courageous act, an act of rebellion that would encourage other such acts. Like Kate Millett, I knew that what I wanted to do as a lesbian and a feminist writer was to remake the world into a place where the truth would be hallowed, not held in contempt; where silence would be impossible.

Sometimes it seems that all I want to add to her philosophy is the significance of craft, a restatement of the importance of deeply felt, powerful writing versus a concentration on ethnography, or even a political concentration on adding certain information to the canon—information about our real lives that would make it possible for lesbians, working-class runaways, incest survivors, and stigmatized and vilified social outlaws to recognize themselves and their experiences. If I throw everything out and start over without rhetoric or a body of theory behind my words, I am left with the simple fact that what I want as a writer is to be able to tell the truth so well and so powerfully that it will have to be heard, understood, and acted on. It's why I have worked for years on lesbian, feminist, and gay publishing, for no money and without much hope, and why my greatest sorrow has been watching young writers do less than their best because they have no concept of what good writing can be and what it can accomplish.

I started this whole process—forcing my students' discussion of the good and the bad—in order to work on my own judgment, to hold it up to outside view. I can take nothing for granted with these twenty-year-olds, and there is always at least one old-line feminist there to keep me honest, to ask why and make me say out loud all the things I have questioned and tried to understand. Sometimes it helps a lot. Sometimes it drives me back down inside myself, convincing me all over again that Literature belongs to the Other —either the recognized institutions or my innocent students who have never known my self-conscious sense of sin, my old loss of faith. They question so little, don't even know they have a faith to lose. There are times I look at my writing and despair. I cannot always make it the story I think should be told, cannot make it an affirmation or anything predictable or easy or sometimes even explainable. The story tells itself, banal or not. What, then, is the point of literary criticism that tells writers what they should be writing rather than addressing what is on the page?

The novel I am working on now seems to be driving me more crazy in the actual writing of it than it ever did when I was trying to get around to the writing of it. I don't understand if it is just me or the process itself, since many other writers I have talked to are noncommunicative about the work of writing itself. Everyone discusses day jobs, teaching, what they read, music, being interviewed, groups they work with, things they want to do when this project is finished.

But over here, I am halfway done with the thing and feel like I have nothing, know nothing, am nothing. Can't sleep, and part of the time I can't even work, staying up till 4:00 or 5:00 in the morning. Thinking. About what, people ask, the book? I stare blankly, sometimes unable to explain and other times too embarrassed. I think about the book, yes, but also about my childhood, my family, and about sex, violence, what people will ask me when they read this book, about my ex-girlfriends and what they will say, about my hips and how wide they have become, my eyesight that is steadily growing worse, the friends who have somehow become strangers, even enemies, the friends who have died without ever managing to do the things they wanted to do, how old I have gotten not recognizing that time was actually passing, about why I am a lesbian and not heterosexual, about children and whether the kind of writing I do will endanger my relationship to my son—allow someone to take him away from me or accuse me of being a bad mother—and about all the things I was not told as a child that I had to make up for myself. When I am writing, I sink down into myself, my memory, dreams, shames, and terrors. I answer questions no one has asked but me, avoid issues no one else has raised, and puzzle out just where my responsibility to the real begins and ends. Morality and ethics are the heart of what I fear; that I might fail in one or the other, that people like me cannot help but fail to show true ethical insight or moral concern. Then I turn my head and fall into the story, and all that thinking becomes background to the novel writing itself, the voices that are only partly my own. What I can tell my students is that the theory and philosophy they take so seriously and pick apart with such angst and determination is still only accompaniment to the work of writing, and that process, thankfully, no matter what they may imagine, is still not subject to rational determined construction.

A few years ago, I gave a copy of a piece of "fiction" I had written about incest and adult sexual desire to a friend of mine, a respected feminist editor and activist. "What," she asked me, "do you want from me about this? An editorial response, a personal one, literary or political?" I did not know what to say to her, never having thought about sorting out reading in that way. Certainly, I wanted my story to move her, to show her something about incest survivors, something previously unimaginable and astounding—and not actually just one thing either, as I did not want one thing from her. The piece had not been easy for me; not simple to write or think about afterward. It had walked so close to my own personal history, my night sweats, shame, and stubborn endurance. What did I want? I wanted the thing all writers want—for the world to break open in response to my story. I wanted to be understood finally for who I believe myself to be, for the difficulty and grief of using my own pain to be justified. I wanted my story to be unique, and yet part of something greater than myself. I wanted to be seen for who I am and still appreciated—not denied, not simplified, not lied about or refused or minimized. The same thing I have always wanted.

I have wanted everything as a writer and a woman, but most of all a world changed utterly by my revelation. Absurd, arrogant, and presumptuous to imagine that fiction could manage that—even the fiction I write which is never wholly fictive. I change things. I lie. I embroider, make over, and reuse the truth of my life, my family, lovers, and friends. Acknowledging this, I make no apologies, knowing that what I create is as crafted and deliberate as the work of any other poet, novelist, or short story writer. I choose what to tell and what to conceal. I design and calculate the impact

I want to have. When I sit down to make my stories, I know very well that I want to take the reader by the throat, break her heart, and heal it again. With that intention, I cannot sort out myself; say this part is for the theorist, this for the poet, this for the editor, and this for the wayward ethnographer who only wants to document my experience.

"Tell me what you really think," I told my friend. "Be personal. Be honest." Part of me wanted to whisper, Take it seriously, but be kind. I did not say that out loud, however. I could not admit to my friend how truly terrified I was that my story did none of what I had wanted—not and be true to the standard I have set for myself. Writing terrible stories has meaning only if we hold ourselves to the same standard we set for our readers. Every time I sit down to write, I have a great fear that anything I write will reveal me as the monster I was always told I would be; but that fear is personal, something I must face in everything I do, every act I contemplate. It is the whisper of death and denial. Writing is an act that claims courage and meaning, and turns back denial, breaks open fear, and heals me as it makes possible some measure of healing for all those like me.

Some things never change. There is a place where we are always alone with our own mortality, where we must simply have something greater than ourselves to hold onto— God or history or politics or literature or a belief in the healing power of love, or even righteous anger. Sometimes I think they are all the same. A reason to believe, a way to take the world by the throat and insist that there is more to this life than we have ever imagined.

### JEWELLE GOMEZ
## from Because Silence Is Costly

> I have come to believe over and over again that what is most
> important to me must be spoken, made verbal and shared,
> even at the risk of having it bruised or misunderstood. That
> the speaking profits me; beyond any other effect.
>> —Audre Lorde, "The Transformation of Silence
>> into Language and Action," in *Sister Outsider*

To speak of who we are as African-Americans has traditionally been a sign of triumph over adverse conditions. It
was the telling of how we rose "up from slavery" into freedom and independence. It was a tale told in the early
narratives of former slaves collected while other Black
women and men were still held in bondage in this country.
And in letters, magazine articles, and autobiographies written by African-Americans during the past two centuries.
This tale of survival was and still is told around the kitchen
tables of Black Americans in banter, jokes, in song and
legend. And, most exquisitely, it is written in the fiction
that Black women and men have been creating almost as
long as we have been sharing our oral histories.

To speak of who we are as Black lesbians and gays is
equally as urgent and as triumphant a story, one whose
telling has been somewhat more guarded. To say you are a

lesbian or gay man to your family, friends, or co-workers is made difficult by a number of factors that have raised coming out (that process of speaking who we are) from a simple declaration into an important rite of passage. The psychological, social, and biblical misinformation dominating heterosexual assessment of lesbian/gay life makes coming out a nightmare for many of us, regardless of ethnicity. My own was unusually rewarding: my family responded as thinking, loving people, not as heterosexuals gripped by fear. The only pain was in the years before I was actually able to speak the words aloud. But other reactions vary—threats of (and actual) institutionalization, physical violence, ostracizing one's partner, rejection from the family. And because of a presumption of heterosexuality in this society, coming out is a process which must be repeated over and over again.

In the telling of our lives as African-Americans, being lesbian or gay was not something to "speak on." It did not fit the social picture of normality African-Americans wished to project in order to combat racist stereotypes. Nor did it suit the political strategies outlined by church and civil rights leaders for liberation.

Nevertheless, an individual's need to come out of the closet and name her/himself sexually is not only part of a political strategy but is, more fundamentally, at the core of accepting adulthood and validating one's own experience. Coming out is not merely announcing a personal choice to the world, it is a step in accepting your identity. For Black lesbians/gays it means saying both *I am gay* and also declaring *I am still Black*.

The coming-out story has acted as a major unifying thread in a lesbian/gay community that is as diverse as the United

States itself. At any women's bar, or lesbian caucus, or lesbian and gay film festival, the participants represent a cross section of America, embracing divergent class, political, and ethnic identities. This diversity, which has been an important part of the strength of the Movement, also makes it difficult to maintain coalitions. A reinterpretation of the traditional coming-of-age story, the coming-out story has been the one bond that touches all. Everyone, whether already out or deeply closeted, is able to discuss the experience of sharing their life choice. It becomes a linguistic currency that allows all lesbians and gays at least one place in which they can identify with each other. As such, it also places Black lesbians and gays in conflict with Black culture where it is considered a risk to the entire community to say such things aloud.

The coming-out story occupies an important place in African-American letters for several reasons. First, its genesis in a political movement, as well as its frequent practice by nonwriters and professional writers alike, are significant literary factors, much as they were when slave narratives were being collected, or during the Black Arts movement of the 1960s. Second, and perhaps most interesting, is the close relationship the coming-out story has to the pure oral tradition of African-Americans and the slave narratives of the nineteenth and early-twentieth centuries. It preserves the natural speech patterns of the one who is telling the story, and is usually a tale of triumph over repressive conditions in which the narrator emerges with a stronger, more positive identity. The emphasis in coming-out stories is, as is often true in autobiographies and slave narratives, on the importance of the story itself rather than the literary form in which the story is conveyed. It captures the irony, wit, and wisdom frequently exhibited in traditional African-American storytelling. And it is through the interview or oral narrative that the stories of those who do not consider themselves writers are best recorded, giving a truer reflection of the breadth of the Black lesbian and gay community.

The Black coming-out story continues to evolve in a variety of forms. The overriding theme and focus of these stories is a reconciliation of gay lifestyles with Black identity, a regaining of a sense of wholeness within oneself and with one's Black community. But any move toward this reconciliation must always confront the peculiar position the Black community has historically held regarding sex. In her article, "The Failure to Transform: Homophobia in the Black Community," Cheryl Clarke points out:

> We have expended much energy trying to debunk the racist mythology which says our [Black] sexuality is depraved. Unfortunately, many of us have overcompensated and assimilated the Puritan value that sex is procreation, occurs only between men and women, and is only valid within the confines of heterosexual marriage.[1]

The growth of the women's movement, following on the energy of the Civil Rights movement in the 1960s and in tandem with the Anti-War movement of the seventies, provided a crucial opportunity for Black women to explore their lives, history, and art. Despite the repressive attitude toward public discussion of sex and gender in this country, such movements inevitably led to the exploration of sexuality and heterosexual roles for both women and men. Before "outing" became a political tool and a way to sell magazines, activists extolled the virtues of coming out as a serious political and personal action. But outing was always a tactic favored in some quarters.

Such was the case with civil-rights leader Bayard Rustin as he organized the historic 1963 March on Washington. Speaking in a newspaper interview in 1987, Rustin recalled:

> Then Strom Thurmond stood in the Senate speaking for three-quarters of an hour on the fact that Bayard Rustin was a homosexual, a draft dodger and a communist. Newspapers all over the country came out with the front-page story. Mr. [A. Philip] Randolph waited for the phone to ring. And it did indeed ring.[2]

Rustin indicates in that article and others that his sexual orientation was always known among the political leaders with whom he worked, including Mr. Randolph, Martin Luther King, Jr., and Roy Wilkins. In 1960 Rustin had agreed to step down as an adviser to Dr. King when it was suggested that his participation might jeopardize any effort King led. Rustin was nevertheless charged with organizing the 1963 march. He indicates that the accusations of homosexuality were lost, a response Thurmond could not have anticipated, among those of draft evasion (Rustin, a Quaker, had spent three years in prison as a conscientious objector) and communism (he had been a socialist). Although Rustin received support from both Randolph and King, his public presence diminished greatly after the Strom Thurmond attack. Before his death in 1987, Rustin worked quietly with the A. Philip Randolph Educational Fund and contributed his support to gay organizations such as Men of All Colors Together and the National Coalition of Black Lesbians and Gays. His sentiments on coming out were unequivocal: "Every Gay who is in the closet is ultimately a threat to the freedom of Gays…. Remaining in the closet is the other side of prejudice against Gays."[3]

On the other hand, for renowned blues singer Alberta Hunter, the idea of coming out publicly as a lesbian was unthinkable. The distinct difference between her feelings and those of Bayard Rustin may, in part, be explained by their age difference (she was probably more than ten years his senior). But upbringing was certainly an important factor.

The strongest impulses that Hunter, also a songwriter, with material recorded by singers such as Bessie Smith, appears to have followed throughout her life and career were establishing financial security and promoting an air of personal propriety. A friend, Harry Watkins, recalls that Hunter "even had Confederate Dollars. That's how much she saved money!"[4] And Hunter certainly learned strict lessons at home about modesty. She recalls that when growing up in Memphis she was not allowed to go barefoot even inside her house. Her sense of privacy, which was certainly a by-product of such upbringing was reinforced by some of her friends. Watkins, being interviewed for Hunter's biography after her death, when questioned about her long-lasting affair with Lottie Tyler, refused to comment. "He rolled his eyes and sang a few lines of 'T Ain't Nobody's Business If I Do'."[5]

Despite her growing popularity in the United States and Europe, Hunter guarded her personal relationships with women with a tenacity most others, like comedian Jackie "Moms" Mabley, refused to bother with. A ladylike presence was imperative to the persona Hunter created on the stage and to her own sense of self. In her biography, she expresses her reluctance to sing on the infamous Beale Street in New

Orleans. This attitude helped to isolate Hunter within the context of her relationships from a community of women who were less closeted than she. According to her biographers, "Alberta was a lesbian...but did everything to conceal this preference all her life. In her mind lesbianism tarnished the image of propriety and respectability she struggled so hard to achieve."[6] No doubt the perceived threat of losing her audience was a major factor in her concern about exposure. Ironically, by the time Hunter made her triumphant comeback in the 1970s, her lesbianism was legend and drew an entirely new audience of young women who came to see a part of lesbian history, sitting side by side with those who remembered her from her earlier career.

> ...in the open fact of our loving
> with not only our enemies' hands
> raised against us
> means a gradual sacrifice
> of all that is simple
> dreams...
>                          —Audre Lorde[7]

One of the first Black lesbians to freely identify herself as such is Anita Cornwell, who published fiction and articles in *The Ladder,* the lesbian journal originally produced by the Daughters of Bilitis. The publication amazingly survived the McCarthy era. Episodes in Cornwell's coming-out story are collected in her book, *Black Lesbian in White America.* The six chapters written in the third person relate Cornwell's initially secret relationship with her first woman lover, Zelmar, who seems to straddle both the lesbian and straight worlds. At the start, Cornwell's only connection with women in a lesbian context is her relationship with Zelmar, but she is aware of the gap already opening between her and her past life:

> Emotionally, she [Anita] was still trapped within the wall she had erected around herself long ago when she was unable to fully cope with her environment in any other fashion.... Although her friends were probably unaware of it, Anita was slowly edging away from them. Since the Gay world was unknown to her, however, she was moving into limbo.[8]

While the relationship with Zelmar opens Cornwell to other relationships with women, it is not until much later that she locates a women's community which gives her a certainty of identity and the promise of a fulfilling life as a lesbian.

When Cornwell began writing this material (1972), Ann Allen Shockley's novel, *Loving Her*, the first explicit and sympathetic book about a Black lesbian, was still two years in the future. In that light, Cornwell remains the first visible Black lesbian activist, and her work is designed as a documentation—much as the slave narratives recorded in the early twentieth century were.

Another coming-out story that is also essentially a documentation is that of Mabel Hampton, which appeared in the *Lesbian Herstory Archives Newsletter*. It is a transcribed oral presentation, including a question-and-answer segment done by Hampton, who was born in 1902. Its charm lies in its immediacy and Hampton's sparkling personality. The beginning is a long narrative describing her running away from home at an early age and being raised in Jersey City, New Jersey. It blossoms, though, when Hampton describes her life as a dancer, and meeting Lillian, who was to become her life partner for over forty years:

In 1932 I was on Lexington Avenue waiting for the streetcar. There were streetcars in those days and a girl says "Are you going..." She was just my height. She said, "Are you going uptown?" I said "Yes." She said "You gonna catch the car?" I said "I'm gonna catch the streetcar." So she says "All right I'm going to too." I looked her up and down and said to myself, goodness gracious, this is a good-looking chick. I said, I wonder if she's in my life, because you see I had danced on the stage and knew all the answers.[9]

The final part of the story is in the form of questions and answers in which specific inquiries are made about nightspots the women who were "in the life" (lesbians) visited and other elements of Hampton's social life. When asked how old she was when she came out, Hampton responds: "Well, I must have come out when I was eight years old. To tell the truth I never was in so I must have been out."[10]

The oral form captures Hampton's turn of phrase, sense of humor, and playfulness, and with it more of the essence of the Harlem Renaissance and the Depression eras. It also gives insight into the postwar period when Hampton had retired from the stage and worked as a cleaning woman in New York City. Her particularly inclusive manner of narrating, capturing colloquialisms of the period and providing physical details, gives her story a very broad perspective.

> Leave my eyes     alone
> why should I make
> believe this place entirely
> is white
> and I am nothing...
> —June Jordan[11]

In 1979, the same year I came out to my mother and grand-

mother in a Times Square movie theater, *Essence* magazine
published the coming-out story of Chirlane McCray:

> When I decided to write this article, I said, "I'm writing this
> for my gay sisters…" As I wrote and relived the pain, I real-
> ized that the fears, which I had assumed to be gone, were still
> within me.… I worry that no employer will hire me again,
> that my free-lance writing assignments will dwindle, that my
> gay friends who are still in the closet will disassociate them-
> selves from me. I fear, in sum, that the monster of conformity
> will rear its angry head and devour me.[12]

Her father's response, "You're Black and you're a woman…
I don't see why you want to be involved in something like
this,"[13] echoes a common attitude among some in the Black
community. The fallacy that homosexuality is "white" has
been used frequently to try to shame Black gays into "recant-
ing."

Neither of McCray's parents was wholly approving, but
she was not met with hatred or reprisals. This reaction certainly played a part in enabling her to publish her
coming-out story under her own name in a national magazine. Her purpose—to offer an example to those living in
isolation—could not have been better fulfilled than by writing in a glossy fashion magazine marketed to the
mainstream population of Black women, many of whom
might never have the courage to look for a lesbian community.

*Essence* had, in an earlier (June 1978) issue, published an
interview with Lea Hopkins, who was identified as the first
Black *Playboy* bunny, from Kansas City, Missouri. At the
time of the interview Hopkins was no longer working as a
bunny or a model, but was active in the Missouri lesbian

political community. The interview was, unlike a coming-out story, a glossy magazine profile. It avoided any lengthy discussion of emotional or political issues. Although the piece was not sensationalistic, the focus was on Lea Hopkins as a startling phenomenon rather than on the impact of her personal journey. Her lesbianism could well have been skydiving, yak farming, or any hobby Blacks don't "usually" do. McCray's first-person account assumes the social and political importance of her information and disallows any shock value her discussion might have.

In 1991, *Essence* magazine published another coming-out story, this one written by *Essence* editor Linda Villarosa and her mother, Clara Villarosa, a bookseller.[14] Using alternating narratives between daughter and mother, each expresses their expectations and disappointments with the roles they've been assigned. With the emphasis this time on the mother's coming to terms with her daughter's orientation, it is almost Clara Villarosa's coming-out story as much as it is Linda's. The article acknowledges that coming out is a growing-up process, and that in order for it to work both the lesbian or gay child and her/his parents and friends must share in the experience. The Villarosa coming-out story more clearly places the lesbian experience within the context of a Black family. Both daughter and mother explored what the process was of coming to terms with their identities (lesbian and mother of a lesbian) more easily within that realm, a perspective offered by few coming-out stories. It is a coming out made possible only by the hundreds of others that came before it....

The 1980s saw the publication of the first full-length coming-out stories by Black writers, Audre Lorde's *Zami: A New Spelling of My Name* (1982) and Larry Duplechan's *Blackbird* (1986), in which a broader range of issues are addressed.[15] Each offers that important perspective of speaking from both inside and outside a Black community in a distinctive voice. The stories occur in different time periods and different parts of the United States, but each testifies in a similar way to the endurance of Black consciousness and the ability to integrate the many aspects of one's personality and create a whole person....

▲▼▲

In view of the difficulty the Black community has had with the imagery assigned to our sexuality, as well as its ambivalence about the role of those with nontraditional (i.e., not white middle-class perceptions of) sexual lives, it is significant that Lorde chooses to treat the sexual aspects of her narrative openly. She refuses to equivocate in her coming-out story, never attempting to either ignore her Blackness or to indicate that she is a lesbian in spite of it. She also is able to acknowledge and describe her political perspective on race, gender, and sexuality without relinquishing the specifics of her sexuality as a Black woman and as a lesbian. Lorde's open exploration of the sexual nature of her life is an important departure from the majority of writing by African-Americans, either fictional or autobiographical. *Zami* offers one of the first honest glimpses of Black lesbian sexuality in American literature devoid of a need to place blame or locate causality.

Lorde's celebration of the sexuality essential to her life, and significant in lesbian and gay life generally, is an exciting step in African-American literature. For many years, and certainly in the recent past shadowed by AIDS, gays have often downplayed the role of sexuality in an effort to deflect criticism. In addition, antipornography activists, representing in many cases more repressive elements of feminism, have attempted to set standards for the appropriate and inappropriate depiction of sexuality. This has cast a pall over some members of the creative community who might consider exploring sex in their literary fiction or autobiographical material. Lorde's work is a coming out not only as a Black lesbian but also as a sexual being whose goal is the successful integration of all of these elements of her life.

In an article entitled "The Historical Text as Literary Artifact," Hayden White says, "...histories gain part of their explanatory effect by their success in making stories out of mere chronicles..."[16] Lorde strives to pull her story out of the realm of "mere chronicle" by defining it as a "biomythography." She opens up the autobiography to include the political and historical perspectives she feels are crucial to the telling of her story as a Black lesbian. It also allows Lorde, the poet, to use the lyrical imagery that marks her other writing, imbuing her coming-out story with a mythical quality. Lorde's abilities as a poet and essayist provide her story with the best elements of direct oral history as well as those of historical fiction. With her good ear for dialogue, she captures the powerful turns of phrase which give events immediacy. She also utilizes the dramatic tension that enhances all storytelling, whether traditional or fictional. *Zami* is the most fully realized coming-out story that the gay and Black communities have. It offers a vision of what it means to be *other*, explores the overlapping issues faced by both groups, and makes clear the bonds that will forever bind anyone who is a member of both the gay and Black communities.

The appearance of two full-length works, Lorde's biomythography and Duplechan's fiction, signifies a shift in the perceived value of the coming-out story and its place in the literary canon of African-Americans. Until recently, most coming-out stories were like those of Hampton or Vernon: short pieces reproduced in anthologies. The presumption is that these longer works will appeal not only to those struggling with their own coming-out stories but also to a broad audience interested in history and autobiography and African-Americans.

Anthropologist John Langston Gwaltney, in preparing his book of twentieth-century narratives, *Drylongso,* found that "In black culture there is a durable, general tolerance, which is amazingly free of condescension. for the individual's right to follow the truth wherever it leads."[17] The important accomplishment of the books by Audre Lorde and Larry Duplechan is their success in following the truths of a Black lesbian/gay experience, and their unflinching portrayal of the Black community's varied response, even when it is shameful. Neither book sacrifices the exciting patterns of Black speech, the nuances of Black life in white America, the exploration of the African-American ambivalence about sexual imagery, or the complexity of gender relations in the Black community. Yet both maintain their integrity as gay stories. As narratives, these books do what the Black coming-out story is intended to do: integrate racial and sexual identities in a way that creates a fully realized whole with potential for a positive impact.

In an article on the autobiographical writings of African-

American women, Frances Smith Foster quotes historian
Roy Harvey Pierce:

> "When we come to try to understand our literature in our his-
> tory and our history in our literature,...*we have to* be ready
> to see new forms, new modes, new styles emerging and to
> realize how all that is new results from a particular con-
> frontation of [one] culture made by a particular [person] at
> a particular time." [18]

In coming-out stories it is first the revitalization of traditional forms—storytelling and narratives—that is most
significant. Then it is the emergence of a new form—
biomythography—which contributes to our understanding
of our literature and our history. The validity of these forms
in African-American culture reasserts itself in the new and
the old voices which essentially tell stories of triumph from
Black gays and lesbians.

Despite the effort of those in the Black community who
have forsaken the tradition of "durable tolerance" that
Gwaltney identified, banishing Black gays and lesbians
from their homes or their literary forums, the coming-out
story reaffirms the legitimacy of the role Black gays and
lesbians continue to play in the Black community whether
they are openly gay or not.

Many writers and editors in the fast-emerging commercial lesbian and gay community have exalted the
development of lesbian/gay writing by saying it is no longer
"just" coming-out stories. In some ways this is true. Lesbian and gay stories have many forms and always will.
From Monique Wittig to Isabel Miller to Nikki Baker, from
John Rechy to John Preston to Melvin Dixon to Assotto Saint,
the stories take us many places besides out of the closet.

But the coming-out story may prove to be the most energetic and engaging aspect of the autobiographical form which is itself experiencing a resurgence in popularity. Biomythography is certainly an exciting genre for creative writers who wish to record their African-American sojourn within the language and emotional scope they've lived it. The blend of history, biography, and poetic spirit seems most suitable for Lorde's need to express both a strong political perspective as well as a highly charged personal account—a need that is familiar to many African-Americans who believe that "what is most important...must be spoken...."

*Black/Out,*[19] the magazine published by the National Coalition of Black Lesbians and Gays, carried four stark words on the cover of one of its issues. They answered the question of why, in spite of fear, Black lesbians and gay men continue to write and speak their coming-out stories. The four simple words are the answer to the why of slave narratives and oral histories handed down to each generation. They tell us why coming-out stories find their niche so comfortably among the stories of all our forebears: Because silence is costly.

## Notes

1. Cheryl Clarke, "The Failure to Transform: Homophobia in the Black Community," in *Home Girls: A Black Feminist Anthology,* ed. Barbara Smith (Albany, NY: Kitchen Table: Women of Color Press, 1983) p. 199.

2. Bayard Rustin, interviewed in the *Village Voice,* June 30, 1987, p. 28.

3. Bayard Rustin, interviewed in *Black / Out,* Vol. I, Nos. 3-4, p. 18.

4. Frank C. Taylor with Gerald Cook, *Alberta Hunter: A Celebration in Blues* (New York: McGraw-Hill, 1987) p. 72.

5. Ibid., p. 7.

6. Ibid., p. 43.

7. Audre Lorde, "Outlines," in *Our Dead Behind Us* (New York: W. W. Norton, 1986) p. 14.

8. Anita Cornwell, "Fleeing the Myths of Motherhood" in *Black Lesbian in White America* (Tallahassee, FL: Naiad Press, 1983) p. 53.

9. Mabel Hampton, "Coming-Out Story," *Lesbian Herstory Archives Newsletter,* No. 7, (1981) p. 32.

10. Ibid., p. 33.

11. June Jordan, "And Who Are You?" in *Things I Do in the Dark* (Boston: Beacon Press, 1981) p. 98.

12. Chirlane McCray, "I Am a Lesbian," *Essence,* September 1979, p. 91.

13. Ibid., p. 161.

14. Linda Villarosa and Clara Villarosa. *Essence,* May 1991, pp. 82, 126.

15. Audre Lorde, *Zami: A New Spelling of My Name* (Watertown, MA: Persephone Press, 1982). Larry Duplechan, *Blackbird* (New York: St. Martin's Press, 1986).

16. Hayden White, "The Historical Text as Literary Artifact," in *Critical Theory Since 1965,* ed. Hazard Adams and Leroy Searles (Tallahassee: Florida State University Press, 1985) p. 397.

17. John Langston Gwaltney, *Drylongso* (New York: Random House, 1980) p. xxvii.

18. Roy Harvey Pierce, *Historicism Once More* (Princeton, NJ: Princeton University Press, 1969) p. 59. Quoted by Frances Smith Foster, "Adding Color and Contour to Early American Self-Portraits," in *Conjuring,* ed. Marjorie Pryse and Hortense J. Spillers (Bloomington: Indiana University Press, 1985) p. 25.
19. Cover caption, *Black/Out,* Vol. 1, Nos. 3–4, 1987.

## TERRY CASTLE
## First Ed

First, Ed—who, for all the sense of drama her memory evokes, is surrounded with a certain haze, a nimbus of uncertainty. Did our encounter, the one I remember, take place in 1963 or 1964? It must, I think, have been 1964, if only because the Dixie Cups' "Chapel of Love" (a crucial clue) was on the radio that summer, lilting out of dashboards all over San Diego, along with "Don't Worry, Baby," "Pretty Woman," and "I Want to Hold Your Hand." It was the summer that my father's large brown-and-white Oldsmobile got a cracked block from the heat, and his hair, which had gone gray after my mother divorced him, went completely white, like Marie Antoinette's. A few months later, the Dodgers, resplendent with Koufax, won the World Series, and I and my fellow sixth-graders, transistors in hand, celebrated with loud huzzahs on the rough gravel playgrounds of Whittier Elementary School.

All during the long hot months of vacation, I went once

a week for a swimming lesson at the old YWCA downtown at Tenth and C Street. We had recently returned (my mother, my younger sister, and I) from two years on the English coast, where we had lived in a gloomy village near Dover. My British-born mother had taken us there—in a flurry of misguided nostalgia and emotional confusion—immediately after her divorce in 1961; and we had stayed on, in a strange state of immobility and shared melancholia, until mid-1963. In the summer of 1964, however, things seemed better. While my sister and I reaccustomed ourselves to the unfamiliar sunshine, my mother exulted in being back in California, in living as a "bachelorette" (with two children) in the pink Buena Vista Apartments, and in the hope—not yet dashed by various Jamesian revelations—of her imminent marriage to the handsome Chuck, the mustachioed ensign in the Navy with whom she had committed the sweetest of adulteries before her divorce.

My mother had been a swimming instructor for the Y during the ten years she had been married to my father, and the organization kept her loyalty, being associated with water, freedom, light, pools, and "living in San Diego"—with everything, indeed, that she had dreamed of as a teenager working for the gasworks in St. Albans. She herself had taken a number of classes at the downtown Y: the intermediate and advanced swim course, synchronized swimming, and beginning and advanced lifeguard training, during which she learned to divest herself of numerous layers of clothing, including laced snow boots, while submerged in eight feet of water. Despite my mother's demonstrated aquatic skills, however, I adamantly refused to let her teach me any of them, and remained, at the relatively advanced age of ten, a coy nonswimmer. After several abortive sessions at the bathroom sink, during which she tried to make me open my eyes under water, it became clear that I was not going to learn anything under her tutelage, but would require instruction from some more neutral party. Hence my introduction to the Y, the children's evening swim program, and the delicious orchestrated flutterings of breast, elbow, and ankle.

The YWCA was an antiquated building by southern California standards—Julia Morganish, from the teens or twenties, though not a work of her hand. It preserved the dowdy grandeur of turn-of-the-century California women's buildings, manifest in its square white facade, Mission-style touches, and cool, cavernous interior. Of the actual decor of the building, I remember little: only, vaguely, some seedy fifties leatherette furniture parked at odd angles in the reception area, peeling bulletin boards, the ancient candy machine expelling Paydays and Snickers with a frightful death rattle, and the small front office staffed—inevitably—by a middle-aged, short-haired woman in slacks. The place had an interesting air of desolation: various lost or ill-fitting souls lingered in the front area especially—off-duty sailors, people speaking Spanish, Negroes and Filipinas, mysterious solitary women. I never saw any of the guest rooms, and did not know that they existed: it would not have occurred to me that anyone might actually live there.

The indoor pool was deep in the netherworld of the building, seemingly underground—a greenish, Bayreuthian extravagance, reeking of chlorine and steam. Entering from the women's locker room, one found oneself immediately at one of the pool's deep-end corners. A wobbly diving board jutted out here in dangerous invitation, while at the opposite end a set of pale scalloped steps beckoned to the less adventurous. Running around the pool on all sides was an ornate white tile gutter, cheerfully decorated—by the same wayward deco hand, presumably, that had done the steps— with tiny mosaic flowers and swastikas. The water itself was cloudy, awash with dead moths and floating Band-Aids, but nonetheless, in its foggy Byzantine way, also warm- seeming and attractive. A slippery tiled walkway, inset with more flowers and swastikas and the imprinted words DO NOT RUN, completed the scene. Along this elevated plat- form our blond-haired teacher, an athletic woman named Pam, would slap up and down in bathing suit and bare feet, calling out instructions in a plaintive Midwestern tongue.

We were five or six in all, a sprinkling of little girls in cotton suits with elastic waists, and one or two even smaller boys in minuscule trunks. Under Pam's guidance, we soon mastered the basics: the dog paddle, a variety of elementary crawls and backstrokes, flapping sidestrokes, "sculling" and "treading water"—all with much gasping and excite- ment. It was on one of these occasions, while struggling to float on my back without inhaling water, that I must first have seen Ed. The ceiling over the pool was high up, some thirty or forty feet, with tall windows of opaque glass near the roof line, through which a few dim green rays of evening sunlight would sometimes penetrate to the fluorescent fug below. A dusty balcony overhung the pool at this level, stacked with seldom-used folding chairs for the spectators who came to observe the water-ballet displays put on by the synchronized swimming class. Ed stood up there aloft, along with a few seamen in whites, waiting for the adult free-swim hour that immediately followed our class.

Even from my unusual angle I could see that Ed was

spectacularly good-looking—in a hoodish fifties way that had not yet, by mid-1964, been utterly superseded by the incoming styles of the era. I might grace my bedroom bulletin board with the toothy images of John, Paul, George, and Ringo, but Ed's "look" (as I knew even then) was far more compelling. Indeed I felt oddly giddy those times when she met my gaze—as though our positions had reversed, water and air had changed places, and I was the one looking down from above. She wore men's clothes of a decade earlier, Sears, Roebuck style, the tightest of black pants (with a discreet fly), a dark leather belt and white shirt, a thin striped tie, and, as I saw later, the same pointy-toed black dress shoes worn by the Mexican "bad boys" at Clairmont High School, down the street from the Buena Vista Apartments. Her hair was excessively, almost frighteningly, groomed into a narrow, scandalous pompadour, and had been oiled with brilliantine to a rich black-brown, against which her face stood out with stark and ravishing paleness. She appeared to be in her late twenties or early thirties— definitely "old" to me—though something about the drastic formality of her costume also gave her the look of a teenage boy, one dressed up, perhaps, for a senior prom. She spoke to no one, smoked a cigarette, and seemed, despite her great beauty, consumed by sadness. She had a thin face of the sort I would later find irresistible in women.

One evening, more sultry than usual, my mother, who normally dropped me off and picked me up after class in the front foyer, was unable to collect me, owing to some sudden disorder in the radiator of our bulbous green Studebaker. My teacher, Pam, and her mother, the gamy old Peg, a short, tanned woman who wore pants and also taught swimming classes at the Y, agreed to drive me home to

Clairmont in their car. As soon as they had closed up the office, we were to leave.

I had already finished changing and sat by myself in the locker room, waiting for my ride, when Ed came in. The other little girls were long gone. The floor was still wet with the footprints of the departed; the thick, damp air hung about like a dream. At the same time everything seemed to open up, as if I—or she and I together—had suddenly entered a clearing in a forest. Ed said nothing, yet seemed, in some distant way, to recognize me. I sat still, not knowing where to go. She scrutinized me ambiguously for a few moments. Then, as if some complex agreement had been reached between us, she began to strip away, vertiginously, the emblems of her manhood.

Ed, Ed, my first, my only, undressing. She moved gracefully, like a Pierrot, her pallid face a mask in the dim light. She removed her jacket and unbuckled her belt first, laying them carefully on the bench next to me. Then she slipped off her shoes and socks. I gazed down at her bare feet. Her eyes met mine and looked away. Then she loosened her tie with one hand, and pulled it off, followed by her heavy cuff links. Glancing again in my direction, she began to unbutton her shirt, twisting her torso in an uneasy fashion as she did so. She wore, heartstoppingly, a woman's white brassiere. This she unhooked slowly from behind and, watching me intently now, let her breasts fall forward. Her breasts were full and had dark nipples. She stopped to flick back some wet-looking strands of hair that had come down, Dion-like, over her brow. Then rather more quickly, with a practiced masculine gesture, she began to undo her fly. She removed her trousers, revealing a pair of loose Jockey shorts. She hesitated a moment before uncovering the soft hairiness beneath—that mystery against which I would thrust my head, blindly, in years to come. I stared childishly at the curly black V between her legs. She took off her watch, a man's gold Timex, last of all.

Her transfiguration was not complete, of course: now she took out a rusty-looking woman's swimsuit from a metal locker and began, uncannily, stepping into it. She became a woman. Then she folded up her clothes neatly and put them away. Still she did not speak—nor, it seemed, did she ever remove her eyes from mine.

I am aware, too late, how almost painfully sexy Ed was—and perhaps, at the level of hallucination, intended to be. Even now I seem to see the disquieting movement of her chest and shoulders as she leaned over the bench between us, the damp pressed-in look of her thighs when she began to pull the resistant nylon swimsuit up her body, her breasts poignantly hanging, then confined, with the aid of diffident fingers, in the suit's stiff built-in cups. Indeed, I seem to be assisting her, leaning into her, even (slyly) inhaling her. She bends slightly at the knees, balances herself with one hand against the locker, begins to hold me around the neck—but this is a fantasy of the present. In that moment my feelings were of a far more polite, delicate, even sentimental nature. Astonishment gave way to, resolved into, embarrassment. When at last Ed drew on, over the dark crown of her head, a flowered Esther Williams–style bathing cap—the final clownish touch of femininity—I felt, obscurely, the pathos of her transformation: she had become somehow less than herself. But her eyes, with their mute, impassive challenge, never faltered. They seemed to say, I own you now. And I realized, too, though I had no words for it at the time, how much I adored her, and what tumult lay ahead.

The other women came and got me soon enough—Ed must have gone—for the next thing I remember is sitting deep in the well of the backseat of my teacher's Plymouth, the warm night breeze blowing in my face, and the lights of downtown glinting in the background as we drove away. Pam and her mother talked in a desultory, friendly way in the front seat. They used slang with each other and swore softly—almost as if I weren't there, or were much older, which I enjoyed. I looked at the backs of their heads, at Pam's blond nape and her mother's cropped gray thatch, while the sounds of the radio—KCBQ—wafted sweetly through the summer air:

> We're going to the chapel
> And we're
> Gonna get ma-a-a-rried
>
> Going to the Chapel of Love

Then, as we wound our way down 101 through Balboa Park, under the tall bridge by the zoo, the two of them began—as if to the music—to talk about Ed. They seemed to know her; they spoke almost tenderly, referring to her by name. Ed looked more like a guy than ever, my teacher remarked. The words hung about softly in the air. I began listening hard, as I did at school. Her mother, Peg, reflected for a moment, then glanced back and smiled at me in the dark, enigmatically, before murmuring in reply, "Yeah, but she don't have the superior plumbing system." And into the night we sped away.

Many years later, when I had just turned twenty-two, and lay in bed with a much older woman with whom I was greatly in love, I told the story of Ed, this story, for the first time. I was already getting on Helen's nerves by that point;

she tried to find the fastest way through my postcoital maunderings. Ed was, she concluded, "just an externalization." As she often reminded me, Helen had spent fifty-thousand dollars a year for eight years of psychoanalysis in Chicago. She wore her hair in a long braid down her back to represent, she told me, her "missing part." She was thin and dark, and, when she wasn't teaching, wore a man's watch and lumberman's jacket. My mother, she said, "sounded like a hysteric." A lot of things happened later, and I finally got to resenting Helen back, but that's a winter, not a summer, story.

## CAMILLE ROY
## from **South Side**


<New scene; two lovers; possible minimal costume and set change. Lover X can appear to be Gayle. Sound of rain.>

<LoverX>
I felt like I was hitchhiking, since I hardly knew you. Your pickup had a case of beer in the back. We drove up a canyon to your place, an apartment in a weathered turquoise building next to a stand of eucalyptus.

<LoverY>
It's so easy at first. You had a slip. White rags, spread with a butter spoon and soft, spotting under your skin. My tongue lapped your cheekbones, thin as a rail, something to lean over and look out—like on a ship.

<LoverX>
It was twilight, and through the open door the sky was turning a deep blue streaked with smoke.

<LoverY>
You said, *I want to do something for you*. Then you made a mess.

<LoverX>
You treat sex as a combo of rope and past tense.

<LoverY>
It covers your yards of mouth.

<LoverX>
You lick flesh like an envelope.

<LoverY>
**How bad were you today, baby?**

<LoverX>
When your knees press my temples, there's a curly fence near my mouth.

<LoverY>
When I learned about gender, I was very surprised. The proceedings slid from a folder, there were loose papers all over the floor.

<LoverX>
Before that, you only experienced animals.

<LoverY>
It's not possible, I thought, after my first lover told me, *Anyone who likes to be fucked is a girl. Anyone who only likes to be fucked is a woman.*

<LoverX>
When I was fifteen, my sister June told me I shouldn't have sex until my nipples turned brown. I figured she thought that would never happen. She was three years older, kept her drugs and sex in the basement the same way she kept her jewelry there. Her lovers were thin white men whose troubles were drug related. When Paul got out of Cook County Jail, he carried an odor of rape and there was fear in his eyes, I could feel that in my stomach when he was around; otherwise I didn't care.

<LoverY>
I thought about Monica: her sharp teeth and brown cheeks. The way her greed slid across my hips could be scary but her palms were narrow as slots, that made it okay to have sex with her. Monica was black in a segregated city; so the closer I got the more transparent I became, my exact longing vicious as the wavering light of association.

<LoverX>
It shut me up.

<LoverY>
The soot where we're the same, rolling downhill on a boulevard lined with palm trees and novelty shops...

<LoverX>
At sixteen I saw it this way: there's only one city like there's only one big fist.

<LoverY>
Aggression is just a manner of speaking, conversation taking shape.

<LoverX>
I'm shielding my cigarette from the wind while I try to remember where I live; on a block that slides uneasily from white to black. It's one A.M. and the snow is falling through a web of fine black particles, soot from the mills. Monica is wearing a red T-shirt under her black jacket.

<LoverY>
The streets were deserted after dark, and any stranger carried death!

<LoverX>
We've just come out of the basement. We started out watching each other, lips back, drinking beer. Where our skin slides together along the damp basement wall, there's a streak of feeling like a welt. I open another beer, to sink this awful strangeness. Then her palms are warm and under my jaw, sliding back around my head. That's okay, so I peel off her T-shirt. It is very interesting how dark her nipples are. I touch them with my fingers and then my lips. Then I lean back, feeling thin as a sheet. I'm washed out, ripped. She kisses me clear to the back of the throat, where the tongue splits. I figure I don't know anything but she's an excerpt from another life.

<LoverY>
You mark time backward to the moment of damage.

<LoverX>
I eroticize dread.

<LoverY>
I was thirteen the first time Monica brought me home, and
I sat on a yellow chair next to the television. The plaid
couch was covered with sisters with white teeth and dark
skin, laughing at me I thought. But I was happy there, listening to the radio: WVON, Otis Spann the Blues Man,
coming from the kitchen.

<LoverX>
You *liked* the closed-in feeling. Every relation defined
through position and abandonment.

<LoverY>
Monica's apartment building had the windowsills painted
yellow; they were speckled with grit from the steel mills. The
rooms were hot, or full of the weather whatever it was, and,
leaning out over the sills, I saw stone pots of geraniums at
the door. We watched the street. The drunks were tall and
moved like wavy reeds. They followed Melinda in her flowered housedress, Melinda who hacked when she laughed
and whose crooked eyes bulged out in two directions. Her
stomach rose and split every year with a new kid.

<LoverX>
In the frustration of matching myself to the present, I'm
always missing something.

<LoverY>
I'm shy about death.

<LoverX>
It's September, and Monica walks into school with her fingers loosely rolled and a snap in her stride. Between classes we're kept in formation, thin lines of skittish kids on opposite sides of the wide hall. There are green iron bars over the windows, the walls are dark red brick and gray stone. Gang wars edge in over the cracked pavement of the schoolyard. September is still summer; there's that other kind of light. Thicker, concentrated. There's weeds in the sidewalk cracks, gardens in vacant lots. Monica is light on her feet, agile. I take her curled lip to follow; I want to please. I make it obvious. She says, *Sorry didn't do it, you did,* and laughs. Like she does when she tells me about the death. Even I know that's wrong, to laugh at her daddy, dragged out of his taxicab, dead of a heart attack at forty-four. It's late September, the two of us stand by the window in an empty classroom, the sky is a dull blue. When I tell her to quit laughing, she wipes a smile on and runs out of the building. She got poorer after that, had to move out of the district.

<LoverY>
With you I felt no guilt. I was willing to do almost anything for that.

<LoverX>
I got a postcard from my sister. It said:
    Make X mark the beginning of the story. Action, no plot.
I sent one back. It read:
    Y delineates wish.

&lt;LoverY&gt;
*It's my way or the highway, bay-bee.*

&lt;LoverX&gt;
I just wanted to close the mouths of the lovers as they got close to one another, so their aggression is a manner of speaking, conversation taking shape.

&lt;LoverY&gt;
I gave her the word this morning but she can't think about it. She picks up the *Sporting News* as her thoughts plop from one to the other of all the drugs we've got in the house. She's thinking about the heroin in the basement.

I like hallucinogens and she likes opiates; one of our differences.

&lt;LoverX&gt;
She has the soft round eye of a calf—that's misleading. And perfect pouty lips. It was a really bad sign when she painted them red before 9:30 in the morning. I just stared at her lips. A breach—that's what it is. An impossible disruption. Am I on the other side yet?

&lt;LoverY&gt;
I stroked my lips red. Then I leaned toward the mirror, pulled down my eyelid, and drew the short stub of an eye pencil under the lashes, making a thin black line. When I'd done both eyes, I tossed the pencil into the trash. *Another girlfriend gone.*

<LoverX>
I can have a white car and drive in the narrative of shadow.

<LoverY>
An elastic grin surfaces under my feet. You're too much for my aching stomach.

<LoverX>
If I left you, I could steal anything.

<LoverY exits>

# 1975: All That Shattered

This was my daughter's idea. She thought I should talk to someone. My husband and I have done very well. We're close to retirement. We've almost paid for our house. I'm a lab tech; my husband is a public-works supervisor for the city.

Our boys live with us, aged sixteen and twenty. Our daughter dropped out of university; she's neither here nor there. I don't know what she's doing. Doesn't really live anywhere. She just got back from Europe. Went on a one-way ticket! She dropped out last year and goes here 'n' there, here 'n' there...Oregon, Washington, Hawaii, I don't even know where, doesn't barely tell us. Now she's thinking of going back to Oregon to live; I don't know what anybody'd want to live there for.... She stays with some kind of group.... I don't know. I don't understand.

They don't get along very well. They don't communicate.

In my day, we were all close: brothers, sisters, cousins, everyone. We were all raised together in one house.

How do they talk to each other? They don't. They don't speak. They avoid each other. It's very distressing.

But last month they had a horrible fight.

My father was in town, he's ninety-three years old, skinny now and frail, but he's sharp upstairs. We went for dim sum in Chinatown one Sunday—Hung Sing on Broadway. I was taking my father's arm, helping him walk; it was packed, the maître d' was leading us to our table. We weren't there more than a minute when I heard this big crash and screaming.

I turned around and it was my sons fighting—socking and punching each other. They crashed over a table by the front window—soup bowls and teacups splashing. One lady was nearly knocked off her chair and another man jumped up as a pot of tea rolled into his lap. The whole restaurant turned and looked, stunned.

The next thing you know they dove through the plate-glass window, head and shoulders first, locked together like animals, hitting and grunting onto the sidewalk. Passersby screamed and old ladies ran for safety. I don't know what exactly happened next, I don't remember, but I saw Winston's head slam against a parking-meter post. It was awful, just awful. My husband came walking up just then, he'd been parking the car, and we pulled them apart to opposite ends of the sidewalk.

Stop it, stop it. What are you doing, I yelled. My youngest was gasping for air, tossing blood out of his eye. His clothes were splattered with green tea and chili sauce.

Grant was cussing, saying terrible things. Pig! I'll kill you! His father clutching him by the arm and the gold-jacketed waiters a head shorter holding him back.

Someone handed me a table napkin and I held it over Winston's eye to stop the bleeding. He had a look in his eye, like I didn't know him. Let me see your head, I said, but he pulled away, fingering his front tooth. I spent a fortune straightening his teeth. I reached to grab his chin to take a look, but he shook me off, glancing real mad at his brother.

Are you OK?

I was crying. After I asked five times, he mumbled something. That's what I mean, they don't communicate.

The restaurant full of people was staring out through the hole in the window, like a giant fish tank of bulging fish eyes. Grant's shirt was ripped and half pulled off his body, his arms all cut.

Then I remembered my dad. Don't move, I've got to get your grandfather, I said. I rushed inside, my dad was standing there shaking on his cane where I left him, in his moss green cardigan and fisherman's hat, his eyes blinking, jaw quivering. Oh, my God, that he had to see this.

*Mat yeh, dim gei,* huh? he wanted to know, gums sliding, his voice raspy and choked.

It's okay, Dad. I pulled a chair over for him to sit down. Just wait. His eyes looked frightened, near tears, madly confused. Just wait till we work this out, I said. What could I say?

My husband paid the owner for the damages, and we took the boys to separate hospitals. First I had to take my father home, I couldn't have him wait in the emergency room for hours. But I wanted to get Winston's head checked right away for a concussion. I dropped off my father at home, had to leave him there alone...it was awful...then took my son to emergency at Mercy. Bo took Grant to St. Luke's by cab.

I asked Winston what happened. He said Grant called him a pig and slammed the door on him as he followed Grant into the restaurant.

You don't hit someone for shutting a door on you or calling you a name, do you? They take things so personally.

Neither of them was hurt seriously, thank goodness. Cuts and scrapes was all. It's very distressing, very distressing. My nerves are nearly shot.

For years my youngest was scrawny. I was real worried about him. Then last year, in the tenth grade, he grew six inches, filled out, real handsome, taller than Grant, even. He bought weight-lifting equipment and started exercising in his room. Just when they're both grown up, they do something so...so childish. This sibling rivalry, you'd think they'd outgrow it.

My philosophy? I've never really thought about it. Well, I don't believe in hitting, if that's what you mean. I work next to the emergency room at the hospital; you walk through a hall of bleeding, moaning accident and fight victims every day and that'll sober you up real quick about driving fast or raising a hand to someone. We get the fallout, and it's no picnic.

When they were kids, I told them if they fight, they should hit only the extremities; don't hit the head, face, or internal organs. And no smoking or drinking. I offered them one hundred dollars if they didn't smoke till they were twenty-one—just like the Kennedys, except they offered one thousand dollars. It didn't work. My daughter smoked in high school, drank some, too, and stayed out late with fellows. Especially this one. What was his name? Paul. He had a sports car and she said he worked at a theater, that's why he kept her out till 3:00 A.M.

The relations between her and the boys? Not so good. But she's gone most of the time now. Went off to school a couple years ago and hasn't come back. She dropped out. My husband and I went away on vacation to the Far East. When we got back, my mother told me Evie had dropped out of U.C. My own mother! Everyone knew, all the cousins, everyone knew except me. It was such a shock! We found her living in the Haight Ashbury. Dancing. I told her it was just a hobby, this dancing, and acting. What happened to Psychology? She was going to be a psychology major. Get a doctorate, get married. Now here she was with these people, dancing. My heart still hurts when I think about it.

Bo and I visited their apartment on Stanyan Street...no furniture. They said they keep the floor clear so they can dance. Everything is alternative. Not chocolate brownies, carob brownies. Not dance, dance movement. Not cold cereal, granola. We had tea and dessert; I said, I don't care how healthy it is, this is not chocolate.

I try to drop hints about returning to Cal. I try to be diplomatic, but I can't help it, it upsets me. Just finish your B.A., I say. She says she's not going back. Why can't she just finish her undergraduate degree? She said that the reason she dropped out is because I complained how much it was costing. Some fight we had spring break, her freshman year. You keep your money, and I'll keep control of my life, she said. What fight? I don't remember any fight. I said no such thing. Other people would be happy to be in her position. One of the finest universities in the world, all expenses paid—it's no skin off her nose.

I worry about the boys, but I worry about her in a different way. This crowd she mingles with. Really odd. For a while she was seeing a lot of this girl at State College; she was typing her papers for her on Freud and she'd say overnight at her house. All her friends now are from the East Coast or up north or somewhere—not from around here. Now she's gone to Europe and come back, and still no plans. Before that it was Oregon. Here and there, here and there, like a Mexican jumping bean.

Once when she was living in Oregon, she visited the house with some of these girls. Scared me half to death. They came at night. Real short hair. Not stylish, but like they were clipped with hedge trimmers. Wore these drapy ponchos and Mao Tse-tung caps, and embroidered patches all over their clothes. Had names like animals and plants. One was named Seaweed and wouldn't talk. She hummed and whistled and made looks with her eyes. Evie said she was a sociology professor! On a talking fast! Now someone explain that to me. They drove these old beat-up vans like hippies at Woodstock on the news. All women. They were all women. Reeked of garlic and not a bra in the crowd. I opened the back door and windows when they left, to air out the house. I couldn't sleep that night, I was so upset.

My husband and I just hope she doesn't do anything permanent. I don't know what a land collective is, but I hope it's not a cult like you read about in the papers. They can't get out, you know, once they join. She's our only daughter. I don't want her to go changing anything.

No, she's not close to her brothers. I told her early on that I would like her to spend more time with the boys, include them in activities, help me out, but she always seemed to prefer the company of her friends. She went to high school, worked part time; at night, she studied and talked on the phone with her friends. Busy. My husband and I both have full-time jobs, and Bo manages apartment buildings on the side. We don't have much time to hover over them; we pretty much let them do as they please. Someone so outgoing, I figured she can spend a little time with her brothers, her own family. It's nothing to her.

Sometimes I've got to bring her down to earth; I tell her I will always be her mother, and she will always be my daughter, I don't care how old we are. I can't let her get too full of herself.

It was hard in the early years. She and Grant shared a room, because at a young age it seemed the boys fought too much; I had to separate them. I moved Winston out to the little sun porch and moved her in with Grant in the second bedroom. My cousin Walt eventually came and built a partition down the center of the floor.

Grant could be destructive. I don't know. Something got into him, he'd cause trouble. He'd come into her side of the room and wreck things, take things. But after a few years we built an addition on the back of the house so each child could have their own room. I thought that worked fine. I was so happy with the addition—it was like having a new house. The supporting beams were massive and strong and upright. The contractors worked a half a year on it. It was even earthquake proof. The hardwood floors were beautiful. Then there was more trouble, so I had to have a locksmith in to put locks on all their bedroom doors. But then there were still complaints. Always something.

What am I supposed to do? He'd been that way since he was a kid—nine, ten years old. Just didn't mingle right, especially at home. Sat in front of the TV morning, noon, and night. Had these outbursts. But don't get the wrong impression...he was a good student, a charming wit, most of the time. He made me laugh, he was so clever. We had high hopes for him.

One time I thought about sending him to military school, or a psychiatrist—but what's that going to do? Cost a lot of money, that's all. If he wants to talk, he can talk to me. I want my children near me. I didn't want to hand them off to some academy to raise, I don't care how good the discipline is. That's what they did in the old days, the old-fashioned Chinese—when a child was born, they shipped it to a wet nurse. My sister-in-law Mabel did that. You avoid the dirty diapers and sleepless nights. I want to raise my own kids, not ship them off.

My husband doesn't have any ideas either. He tried to make Grant happy. Bought him a TV, took him to the movies, out for prime rib. Just the two of them, father and son. Something to make him feel special, because Grant loves meat. Can't get enough of it. He could live on meat alone— no rice, vegetables, just meat. At the dinner table, he gets the best cuts, after his father—sometimes better.

But he hasn't gotten any better...in all this time. I'm tired. I work and come home and take care of the house. Cook and clean and launder and grocery-shop for the family. I don't have the stamina for this. I don't have a lot of hope left...especially after this fight. But I don't have a choice, I have to keep going.

## ROBIN PODOLSKY
# What Can We Make With Fire: What Stories, What Lives?

Art is telling stories. That is to say, art is making reality, is making ourselves. We tell new stories of what we could be. We tell about those things we have to name so they can be shed. This is the twentieth century in America, so we privilege the individual journey, but remember: the individual is a shape-shifting nexus of everybody's story.

The world within which queer artists move is awash with the liquefaction of identity politics; the understanding that we can't pin identity down to an unchanging menu of behaviors or some mythic state of pure being outside the human manufacture of history.

Even as identity politics springs apart—a spray on the lips, a texture and taste, already withdrawing as it grazes the tongue—it pools to a weight big enough to uproot millennia.

Slippery is good. It acts against movement institutions that are internally oppressive, demanding that queers confine their behavior within community guidelines that are at some point arbitrary and which soon become impossible to demarcate anyway. It acts against tendencies for Queer to erase other kinds of identity like class or race or specificity of individual position.

> ...once when I slept with a girlfriend, I had a strong desire to kiss her and... I did do so.... I asked her whether, as proof of our friendship we should feel one another's breasts, but she refused. I go into ecstasies every time I see the naked figure of a woman, such as Venus, for example. It strikes me as so wonderful and exquisite that I have difficulty in stopping the tears rolling down my cheeks.
> If only I had a girlfriend!
> He came towards me.... In a whirl we were clasped in each other's arms.... Is it right that I should have yielded so soon?... I am so lonely—and now I have found consolation.
> —Anne Frank, *Diary*

> The deconstruction of identity is not the deconstruction of politics; rather it establishes as political the very terms through which identity is articulated.
> —Judith Butler, *Gender Trouble*

It's coming to matter less and less whether or not "it" is "genetic" since there's nothing inevitable or "natural" about the categories or meanings that humans generate in regard to biological "facts."

One day my dad, who worked as a meter reader for the Los Angeles Department of Water and Power, was pulled over by a couple of policemen. Both officers approached his car, one on each side. When my father rolled down his windshield, the cop closest to him asked to see his driver's license. He produced it. The cops asked what my father was doing. He said, "I'm working," and reached for the workbook which was next to him in the passenger's seat. Instantly my father found himself staring up the barrel of a gun. There had been burglaries in the neighborhood, and it seemed that my father matched the suspect's description.

"What nationality are you?" demanded the officer.

"I'm an American."

The officer tried again. "What *nationality* are you?"

"I'm Jewish, if that's what you mean."

The workbook was examined and pronounced real. The guns went away. The cops explained that they had made a mistake. The suspect they had been looking for was a "Negro male," driving a Volkswagen. The police had been fooled. They had been misled by irrelevant physical facts: the tightly curled black hair; the thick black mustache; the almond-shaped, brown, almost black eyes; the nose—the product, as was suddenly obvious, not of proximate African roots, but of a two-thousand-year sojourn through an Afro-Semitic, Mediterranean, Asian world which stretched into Eastern Europe and which had brought forth a wide-nostrilled, bulbous, and not at all hooked feature; and, finally, the skin which was—in the descriptive if not the political sense— brown and which, after years of outdoor work, never reddened, but only grew browner.

All of the spurious physical data—genetic accidents which could now be dismissed—had hid an immutable truth. My father's parents had come to this country at the beginning of this century of their own volition. Skin color aside, my father was born an immutably white man.

The cops knew that. They knew it because my father didn't. He knew he was an American. He knew he was a Jew. But he never thought twice, even in the presence of armed police, about what color he was. What better proof of whiteness—historical, political, and immutable—could there be?

In these terms—those through which immutable characteristics are articulated in practice, at gunpoint and under the skin—the nature/nurture debate is off-target. In the solemn game of making identity stories/selves, deconstructionists and essentialists—categories which, long ago, became overdetermined gridlocks of signification—can both play.

He helped to found ACT UP L.A. He drove us crazy with just one more late-night meeting and buoyed us with a smile that said, "Aren't we lucky that we get to have so much fun doing good?" His years of radical organizing brought a tactical maturity to his work that cannot be replaced. He was dead and we were marching through the streets with torches, yelling our guts out.

For some, it was fitting that Mark had died at the height of summer solstice, on bonfire night. He was such a great slut. Solstice would have made Mark himself wince. He wanted nothing spiritual at his funeral, but he did want Lena Horne singing "Stormy Weather," and he wanted lemonade and cookies.

For secular ACT UP people, the torchlight march in Mark's honor continued the tradition of oppressed people moving from victim to fighter, taking rage to the streets. For neopagans, the march was a ritual, the release of a brother's spirit to the flame.

At a crowded intersection, we dropped our torches and made a bonfire in the street. We fed the flames with sheaves of leaflets celebrating Mark's life and mourning his death, with notes that we wrote to him on the spot, with pink triangle ACT UP T-shirts and picket signs. We gave our grief to the fire and our rage; we howled and chanted and held each other. Finally, there was time to cry.

Later, in monogamous bedrooms, in anonymous clubs or in acquaintances' apartments, almost everyone had sex. Later still, we would get together again to fight AIDS.

> ...cultural identity is not a fixed essence at all, lying unchanged outside history and culture.... It is not a fixed origin to which we can make some final and absolute Return. Of course, it is not a mere phantasm, either. It is something.... It is always constructed through memory, fantasy, narrative and myth.... Not an essence, but a *positioning*....
> —Stuart Hall, "Cultural Identity and Cinematic Representation"

Hall isn't talking about queers here, he's talking about Afro-Caribbean people in diaspora. Many movements and peoples are dealing with questions of identity these days. It would be wrong to think about imposing a one-to-one correlation between queer and colonized experiences, as though queers, as a group, had been brought to this continent en masse, tortured and worked for someone else's benefit.

How can we look for one universal queerness "outside history and culture" if our history and culture created what we know of heterosexual norm and created us Outside? In the context of neocolonialism, the danger in our hunt for queer ancestors is in exoticizing and blithely taking over the stories of people whose gender landscape was never ours. How much does the colonizer's hatred of "deviance" unite everyone stamped with that sign?

Because I know this story, I have to tell it: There was a European sailor on one of the first colonial expeditions to what would be called South America. He kept a journal. Here is something he wrote: "The last which was taken and which fought most courageously was a man in the habit of a woman, who confessed that from a child he had gotten his living from that filthiness for which I caused him to be burned."

We find ancestors in strange ways, however we can. A homosexual looking for heritage discovered the writing of a queer-hater who may have been a sodomite. The queer-hater quoted the purported words of a sailor who was part of the colonial expedition.

How much does the answer turn on this possibility: that an erasure, a reflexive refusal, of the bodies of experience and systems of knowledge which are shunted into categories called "psychic," "spiritual," or "metaphysical" is just another Western peculiarity of perception? But, given threads of causality which might span cultures or time, can we trace them back outside of our cultural "lens"?

It can certainly be that social arrangements with features in common like class hierarchies and patriarchy give rise to some common contours in perspective, in how gender and sexuality are organized. What is called male and female, what ways out of the binary are available, what ways out are prohibited and thereby named as possibilities and what chances are available to determined and creative people?

> Contrary to some psychiatric tenets, half and halfs are not suffering from a confusion of sexual identity, or even from confusion of gender. What we are suffering from is an absolute despot duality that says we are able to be only one or the other.... But I, like other queer people, am...male and female....
> —Gloria Anzaldua, *Borderlands / La Frontera*

How do we wield water? The more we flow through the cracks, the more we live in that liminal in-between space, the more we "are ourselves."

I say we come from a place of investment and engagement, or why bother?

We can make identity hold still long enough to formulate a few slogans and demands.

Sure, history is a fiction, that means if we don't retell our own stories, we'll be trapped in the master narrative. Let's take shameless pleasure in reordering our legend. Politically, it's still time to open up more and more queer space. The right wing unblushingly appropriates key tropes of the civil-rights movement (like free speech) in order to roll back that movement's gains; the right wing detonates discursive viruses like Traditional Family Values, which has become a singular noun. Meanwhile, we conscientiously destabilize our own categories, being ever so careful not to totalize

same-gender sexual polarity. How far can we go toward disassembling our own constructions, while those of
heterosexuality remain largely intact? Can we do that without one more time being responsible homosexuals: being
fair, but not treated fairly?

Is *this* the way out: to wallow in the fluidity of our identity, emerging when we choose from that amniotic sea,
born-again pervs, endlessly transforming?

Let's be shape-shifting monsters; let's take the power "they"
give us when they name us demons; let's emerge from our
own mouths as angels with claws.

I have to tell this story because if we don't keep telling, it
never happened. On the night before the March on Washington for Lesbian/Gay/Bi/Queer Rights, there was The
Dyke March. Twenty-thousand lezzies hit the streets by
torchlight, led by an eight-foot gorgon-eyed blue-painted
effigy of Superdyke with a glow-in-the-dark cunt.

When we got to the White House, we fanned out and grew
quiet. And the torchwomen held up their flames and *ate
fire*. They received the fire into their mouths while we
chanted, "The fire will not consume us. We take it and make
it our own." And then the drum women started a rhythm,
women began taking off their shirts, and bare-breasted
dancing dykes passed in front of the White House, in front
of the mounted police, fire in our guts.

Earlier that weekend, a candlelight vigil at the Holocaust
Museum ended with a ritual in which people recited the

names and stories of queers who were burned to ashes. They knew the names of a good number of men, but only one lesbian's name had been preserved.

> ...this other reality, from where we begin to exist, and in which girls again find themselves full of intensity, in the process of project, like an essential force circulating among the spaces.
>
> —Nicole Broussard, *The Aerial Letter*

There's been a problem of separation of the academy from the arts from the streets. We need to work more in service of each other while being adamant about that which our varied perspectives has taught us.

Time to get ruthless about representation, time to work the sphere of popular culture as if fighting for our lives, because we are. We have to mean it. That means let's not be afraid to wield with gusto such problematic formulations as Our Communities, Our Rights, Our Love. Not afraid to put a valorizing frame around the experience of 'ordinary' lesbian/gay/bi/queer people and say these folks are heroes: every time they fuck, every time they come out to the woman at the desk next to theirs, refuse to give up their kids, wear leather in mixed company, get sober, do their first political thing. Each of those moves makes a new story about what it is to be queer, adds a thread to the web of stories that we build to encompass our movement, our emerging culture(s) and yes, let's make it a flexible web, loose, permeable, and always changing.

This is a story I know, so I'll tell it: A bunch of queer artists met in a private home, throwing a party to send one of our bunch to the March on Washington. That man, one of those delightful and exasperating wild-card activists whose particular presence will be impossible to replace, is HIV positive and getting pretty sick. His close friend read a poem about how it might feel when he's not around anymore. There were performances about nursing demented friends, catching blessed moments of hilarity or calm, telling relatives, safe sex, no sex. About facing death with power and grace, with laughter, with kicking and screaming. A lot of the men in the room had HIV. Nobody was over fifty. There was humor and guts and no melodrama, but the air was dense with grief. It needed release.

The evening's climax was a performance in which a man, strapped to a chair, was slowly and lovingly taken through medical procedures which are known to anyone who is or has worked with someone who is HIV positive. The Doctor, in a leather surgical mask, pierced the manacled man with IV needles. He drained him with a catheter and a syringe. As a final flourish, he traced, with a gloved finger, "HIV+" on the patient's chest, using the man's own blood. Some of the spectators were close to tears. Some were excited.

The instruments of medical authority, the disease, the condition of being helpless, the flesh itself—all supposed to be stamped ineluctably as signs of humiliation; things that are supposed to call up fear of retribution and make queer men slough off their bodies in terror were remade/retold into hot, potent tools of queer erotic power.

We will loot the dominant culture for our aesthetic pleasure. We take and discard like the ungrateful brats we are, shamelessly plundering the field of romance for what can serve as bread and seed of an undefined future; destabilizing masculine and feminine while getting off on being both, paring off rot and letting it fall to the transmogrifying earth.

We dare to have valentines and silk stockings, hot wax in the night and tender tongue-touch giggles, pagan rites and the morning paper.

We dare to have it easy whenever we can.

We dare to work like a team of mules when it suits our purpose.

(I will, personally, admit to being a fool for decency, kindness, honor, and grace, those humanist generalizations which are the meat and bones of the very particular nexus of tales that makes me and s/he.)

We dare to make plain talk about honor in crotchless panties.

We are legions of decent working-class girls and boys who claim pleasure as our birthright. Goddess-lovin' mamma's boys, battle-ax dykes, and rootless cosmopolitans: we don't need to hold our parents in contempt, we can carry our ancestors without letting them possess us.

We are each a nexus of refracted signification; we are floods and streams of identity; we are wet, very, very, wet.

No, we're not perfect. We've been known to lie to each other, slap our girlfriends, waste years on alcohol or the illusion of safety. We can quit formulating the impossible burden of being a pure folk, unstained by the dominant culture. Let's get real—every time we reinscribe ourselves, it is with terms we learned at the father culture's knee; we can tell new stories, but most of the words will be old.

Because this story is inside me, I have to tell it: In Salem, Oregon, a Black lesbian named Hattie Mae Cohens and a white gay man named Brian Mock were firebombed in their home by neo-Nazi skinheads. There were eight people in that basement apartment. All of Hattie's young nephews and their girlfriends made it out, but Hattie died of smoke inhalation at the foot of the basement window. Brian was pulled onto the street with flesh hanging off in smoking tatters; he died in the hospital. This happened during a contested state election during which the right wing was trying to pass a state initiative outlawing civil rights for queers. Queer bars were attacked; a church was bombed. Meanwhile, white supremacist skins were doing what they could to incite violence against people of color in Oregon, whose numbers had risen from something like 2 percent of the population to 7 percent. Hattie and Brian's neighbors had been yelling about 'nigger faggots' for weeks; finally one of the nephews had enough and punched a loudmouth whiteboy. Three hours later, Hattie and Brian were burned to death.

Hattie was an old-fashioned bulldagger, dapper in vests and hats. A woman of size. A fixture in the town's one gay bar, she flirted mightily with women and drag queens alike. She was called "Casanova." Also "a lot of fun," "boisterous," "a caring friend," and "dangerous if you got her mad." She was trying to stay out of trouble, saving money to buy a farm with her girlfriend, whom she had met in prison. The girlfriend was still inside when Hattie died. Hattie wrote poems. She always had young people around her: nephews, cousins, and kids from the street whom she was trying to mother into some kind of stability. One of the people who was accused of killing her, a young woman who was acquitted because the guys didn't let her go with them to bomb the house and there was insufficient evidence of her knowledge of the crime, was one of Hattie's special projects.

Brian was a gentle man. He was college educated and a great talker, but sometimes the medicine he took for his schizophrenia slowed him down. He loved to cook with garlic. He made a lot of friends at a community center for mentally disabled people and held discussion groups about homophobia. Hattie had moved in with Brian because, big as he was, he was always being bullied around by local bashers. He didn't fight back because he was afraid he'd hurt someone. Brian weighed close to four hundred pounds. When he was killed, he was still injured from a recent bashing.

This is my life/Why people have to be so ugly/and make people feel anger and different/from another person/They are no better than the next person/We are still people. We have feelings like everybody/I love everybody the same way/We all should be together/We should be the best of friends/I just want to say I love everybody the same way/This, me myself, I mean that from the bottom of my heart.
—Hattie Mae Cohens, poem

Amerika, we are your fucking children, assholes…
—James Carroll Pickett, *Queen of Angels*

We have never had enough space. And on finding it it's like
convergence; you know full well, in that happy posture of
hands on hips, a sexual tenderness that covers all urban
distance…patience and ardour we must constantly renew
in order to make it across the opaque city of the fathers,
always on a tightrope, having to keep our balance, and on all
sides, the abyss. For we work without nets.
—Nicole Broussard, *The Aerial Letter*

What I'm after here is a plea for militant identity that is both
provisional and devout: a plea for allegiance and fervency
along with a willingness to detach from signs of identity
that mark a stage of our oppression.

Let's make art that fucks with narrative structure, disrupt
the linear flow so that our people see our hand and theirs in
making sense of things; let's put impeccably decent lesbians and gays into movie-of-the week melodramas; write
novels about rural organizers who are queer; make poems
about the Goddess; write manifestos that expose and undermine the epistemological operations of all religions; make
Hallmark cards with lesbian/gay fuzzy family units; put
dykeporn on subway walls; reclaim Ruth and Naomi; never
displace our cultural assumptions onto anyone else's story;
fight for the right to marry; put all five of our lovers on our
Kaiser health plans; coach Little League; pierce tits.

Love queer

Love queers

It's time to be about interlocking strategies; to speak in multiple tongues. It's not a question of whether to displace gender or proliferate genders exponentially or organize ourselves into a category of gender which threads backward to neolithic transvestite healing witches, but how to do all of those things effectively and with style.

And, I have to tell this story, because my sisters are burning, my brothers are turning to ash, they who fought most bravely, those harlots turning in the flame, because a stick from Hattie and Brian's house regards me from my desk, because I was there when Chris Brownlie got ruby slippers for his birthday and when he raised his voice at County Hospital and at the Board of Supervisors and in the streets again and again, and there for the silent circle of dykes at his bed, a washing and a laying on of hands, and there when we gave his ashes to the desert, to the sage and oak and the creatures frozen in the great rocks, and if I know this story I have to tell it, so there will be descendants, there will be honoring, and a thread to trace backward so we won't be lost again.

## Works Cited

Anzaldua, Gloria. *Borderlands / La Frontera*. (Spinsters/Aunt Lute, San Francisco: 1987).

Broussard, Nicole. *The Aerial Letter*. (The Women's Press, Toronto: 1988).

Butler, Judith. *Gender Trouble*. (Routledge, NY: 1990)

Cohens, Hattie Mae. Poem in the *Statesman Journal,* Salem, Oregon: September 30, 1992.

Cory, Donald Webster. *Homosexuality: A Cross-Cultural Approach*. (The Julian Press, NY: 1956).

de Guzman, Nuno. The diary of Nuno de Guzman.

Frank, Anne. *The Diary of a Young Girl*. (Washington Square Press, NY: 1963)

Hall, Stuart. "Cultural Identity and Cinematic Representation."

Pickett, James Caroll. *Queen of Angels,* a play presented at Highways Performance Space.

# PAT CALIFIA
## Slipping

A gay man tells me that he thinks lesbians have AIDS envy. It makes him impatient when women talk about safer sex because it isn't really a problem for us. We are, he thinks, just trying to jump on the bandwagon.

I am in Cynthia's kitchen. I have to swallow some aspirin. I take a glass full of water off the table. "That's mine," she says, warning me. "I just drank out of it."

"I know. I don't care."

This is our ritual. When we eat sushi, I dip my tekka maki in her sauce. I steal slices of ginger off her plate. "Don't worry," I tell her. "I don't have a cold. You won't catch anything."

She is my friend. Once she was my lover. She has AIDS. I will not let her drift beyond the world of human touch. I am holding a dental dam over my cunt. It is too wide and not long enough. The rubber sticks to my pubic hair, and when I move the dam around, trying to stretch it tight over my clit, it pulls out a few of my hairs. The woman who is going down on me through the dam is my lover, but we're not getting along. I will have to move out soon. She won't get a job, and I'm tired of paying the rent. This is not sex; it is an experiment. She sucks on my clit, which I hate, but it's the only kind of stroke I can feel through the dam. It reminds me of every bad fuck I've ever put up with in my life, the times I've lain there high and dry in the dark with some-body's mouth working on me, hating her for doing it, hating myself for not responding. When oral sex *does* work, it's sheer bliss, but I am never going to do this again.

I host sex parties for leatherwomen. Only safe sex is allowed. To make this easier, I put out gloves and dental dams and condoms. Before every party, I have to buy more condoms and gloves. But a year later, the original box of dental dams is still full. At least I'm not the only one.

It's Monday. I'm having an argument with Michael, one of the gay men I work with. He's pissed because of an answer I gave somebody in my advice column. I told a reader that giving somebody a blowjob without a rubber was not safe. Michael had a date this weekend with his only steady trick, a man with a really big dick who loves getting sucked. Nor-mally Michael is moody and touchy. Today he's happy, buoyant. He's been smiling all day—until he read my column, that is.

The argument makes me defensive. "I can't tell him to do something that will make him get sick," I protest.

"But a lot of cocksuckers aren't getting sick," Michael says stubbornly.

I start to say something about the long incubation period of AIDS, then I bite my tongue and leave the room. Michael doesn't go to the baths anymore. They've all been closed. He doesn't cruise the parks. He doesn't get fucked anymore. This is what he has left. It makes him happy. And the truth is that if he has a choice between sucking a bare cock and not having any sex at all, I'd rather he got down on his knees and swallowed come. And I hope for his sake that his trick has at least ten inches and comes in pints.

When I first started reading pornography, I was afraid to go into adult bookstores. I bought the paperbacks that you find in regular bookstores under "A" for "Anonymous." Grove Press had reprinted *The Pearl,* a risqué Victorian magazine. At the time, I was in a monogamous relationship with somebody who did not want to have sex with me. *The Pearl* and my newly purchased vibrator were keeping me sane.

I loved all the descriptions of randy uncles plugging their nephews, decadent rakes seducing virgins in private dining rooms, and nuns copulating madly with each other and their father confessors. But there was so much misinformation about venereal disease and pregnancy! People were always employing odd methods of birth control—like douching right after sex—or telling each other they'd been sick last week but were just fine now. There were strange breaks in the narrative. All the female characters would leave England and go to Paris, have their babies, then come home and go straight to the next orgy.

It took me months to figure out why these passages were included. They were the authors' sometimes clumsy way of helping the reader to suspend disbelief, creating an atmosphere in which it was possible to believe that men and women actually felt free to have these ribald adventures. To me, they were anachronisms, but to the intended audience, they were a necessary antidote to perilous times.

Sex has always been a life-threatening experience. Sex has always been a high-risk activity. Because of the pill and penicillin, we forgot that for a little while. But for most of human history, people have had to close their eyes and hope they're lucky before they put it in or let somebody else stick it in.

The Victorian solution to this was to preach a single standard of chastity for men and women. But I have always been on the side of the whores and the rakes. The people who smoked opium, collected pornography, and had illegal abortions. The hustlers and the unfaithful wives. The sailors and their ladies. Colette's waltzing lesbians and passing women, and the street queens who always know everybody's dirty secrets.

I read about the first lesbian case of AIDS in December of 1986. The letter in the *Journal of the American Medical Association* was curt and all the more frightening because it contained so little information. The *Village Voice* ran an article that included a few more personal details. One of the women was dead already. She'd been an intravenous-drug user, had sex with men. The implication was that she was a junkie and a whore. Her lover had ARC. She had not used drugs. She had sex (with condoms) with one bisexual man after getting involved with her female lover. So nobody called her an innocent victim. The two women, the *Village Voice* said coyly, had had "traumatic sex" that caused bleeding.

I wondered who those women were. How did they meet?

Were they Black, Latino, white, Asian, Native American? How long had they loved each other? Did they love each other? Who was taking care of the survivor? Did her family know? What the hell was "traumatic sex," anyway? It sounded suspiciously like something a doctor would say about my sex life. Did either of them own a leather jacket?

On bad days, I don't think safe-sex education is working. I think a few gay men are using condoms, but most of them have just quit fucking. It's probably harder to get AIDS from sucking cock, but by now we've had so much bad news that I can't convince myself that it's safe.

Lesbians still don't believe that AIDS has anything to do with them. The best-educated dykes will grudgingly concede that the disease might be able to pass from one *woman* to another, but not from one real lesbian to another. We already knew that real lesbians don't have sex with men, for fun or for money. But because of AIDS, the pool of women-loving women, pussy-eating, cunt-fucking women who also qualify as "real lesbians" has grown even smaller. Real lesbians don't shoot drugs, share needles, or play sex games that expose them to somebody else's blood. We're all in twelve-step programs, but none of us are junkies. Real lesbians don't sleep with straight women or bisexual women. Real lesbians don't have heterosexual histories.

If a woman has AIDS, she must not be a real lesbian. She's not our problem. We can keep ourselves safe if we don't touch her.

It reminds me of the way good girls never talked to the girls who were easy in high school. As if it were a contagious condition. Girls who got pregnant just dropped out, even if they got married. As if they carried some deadly disease.

I remember the conversations I had with my gay male friends early on, when this disease was still being called "gay pneumonia." All of them wanted very much to believe that only the fist-fuckers were going to get sick.

In the April 23, 1992, issue of the *Bay Area Reporter,* Bo Huston interviewed Sarah Schulman. She's had a lot to say about AIDS since the epidemic began. Some of the dykes I know call her "ACT UP's Poster Girl." Huston asked her, "Okay. This lesbian safe-sex business. What is your position and why are people mad at you?"

She replied, "Well, it's complicated. Somebody in the lesbian community introduced this idea of dental dams, without any substantial discussion—scientific or social—about whether or not they were necessary. And because the community has historically behaved in a very faddish manner, people just went for it. And also because it really fit into a lot of people's shame about their sexuality.

"But the fact is, there isn't any evidence that HIV is transmitted through oral sex between women. And when you look at the four or five cases of women who claim that that was their mode of transmission, the stories don't work. There's always needles or men lurking in the background.

"But, secondly, even if you did have proof that HIV was transmitted through oral sex with women, dental dams have never been tested for efficacy. So we don't even really know if dental dams would inhibit the transmission. Yet people just went on the bandwagon with this thing, and created a climate in which to criticize it meant you were, quote, jeopardizing women's lives, unquote…. If HIV could be spread by oral sex with women, straight men would be getting it, and they're not."

Gay Men's Health Crisis doesn't like dental dams much either. I called their hotline several years ago, when I first heard dams could be used to make rimming or cunnilingus safe. The man who answered the phone said, "Oh, we don't recommend that people use them." When I asked him why not, he told me that one little square of latex wasn't going to prevent anybody from getting contaminated vaginal liquids in his (!) mouth because when women got excited, they began to secrete large quantities of fluid that just went *everywhere*.

Gay Men's Health Crisis has a brochure called "'Women Loving Women." It advises us to "use latex gloves when masturbating" and tells us not to use "plastics such as those used for...household wraps" during oral sex because "Many of these materials also contain toxic chemicals." More toxic than HIV? They've produced one safe-sex audiovisual aid for lesbians, and I can imagine what Jean Carlomusto had to go through to persuade them to produce it. *Current Flow* is a great video that stars Annie Sprinkle and a very hot black dyke named Shara. It's also only five minutes long. A lot of dykes won't watch this movie because Annie Sprinkle is a porn star, and they don't think she has anything valid to say about their intimate relationships.

A San Francisco company that distributes sex-education films, Multi-Focus, has a 22-minute tape called *Latex and Lace* that's described in their catalog as a lesbian safer-sex movie. It features brief interviews with women who talk about AIDS and then shows some of them having a safer-sex orgy. None of them identify as lesbians. Lesbian safer-sex is never defined. Any educator who tried to use this film for a lesbian audience would first have to deal with the negative reactions to straight and bisexual women "pretending" to be lesbians for a sex movie, then cope with the audience's hostile response to the idea that lesbians could have public, anonymous sex with multiple partners.

The San Francisco AIDS Foundation has no movies about lesbians and safer sex. They do have a pamphlet, "AIDS...and Lesbians," which has good information about cleaning needles, plastic wrap, and S/M. But I can't help thinking how many woman-hours have been donated to this organization and others like it. Seems to me we should get something in return besides five minutes of videotape and two pamphlets.

In 1987, Dr. Margaret Fischl at the University of Miami reported that 119 women with AIDS survived for an average of 6.6 months after diagnosis, compared with an average of 12 to 14 months for men with AIDS. She said, "AIDS in women may be a different disease." In 1992, the Centers for Disease Control still refuse to make official a new definition of AIDS that would include the pelvic and vaginal infections that are unique to HIV-infected women as criteria for an AIDS diagnosis.

Lesbians know why gay men get AIDS. It's a natural consequence of male selfishness and dirtiness and violence. A hard cock has no conscience. Men just want to be able to stick their hard dicks anyplace they feel like it. They have no sense of responsibility toward their partners—or themselves. They can't think past an orgasm to its consequences.

Every dyke knows that semen is dirty and vaginas are clean. Menstrual blood can't be equated with the blood in a dirty syringe or scum in a queer boy's butt. If we are at risk—if this clean community of young, attractive, femi-

nist women has been contaminated by a foul male disease—
it's because I and women like me have encouraged other
dykes to imitate men. We've encouraged promiscuity, S/M,
bisexuality, drug use, working in the sex industry.

Of course, all this stuff was happening before, but those
goddamned leather dykes have insisted on talking about
it, and once you label something, you have to admit it's
going on. You have to admit that lesbians are not exempt
from giving each other chlamydia, herpes, trichomoniasis,
hepatitis, even AIDS. You have to talk about the sweaty,
messy stuff that lesbian solidarity is based upon: the sound
of bellies slapping together in the dark, the taste another
woman leaves under your tongue, scrubbing shit out from
under your fingernails, the mean way women sometimes
have of saying no just because you really do want them,
taking her tampon out with your teeth, wondering if buying
a sex toy will save your marriage or make her finally leave
you, thinking about somebody else while she makes you
come, wondering how much longer it's going to take to make
her come, getting wet just because she looked at you.

The essential ingredients of lust are awkward and embarrassing, and they remain the same whether you are into
leather, vanilla, cherry, chocolate, or some other flavor of lesbian sex. There is no such thing as a sexual encounter in
which you don't have to deal with power as well as germs.
It's interesting that the girls who are into exchanging power
are the ones who are the least likely to be exchanging
viruses. If she has handcuffs on her belt, chances are she has
some gloves in her pocket. Prophylactic paraphernalia has
become a new signifier for S/M. In the larger lesbian community, if you ask somebody how she feels about safer sex,
chances are good she also expects you to ask if you can tie

her up. Women who refuse to talk to S/M dykes don't seem to want to talk to each other about AIDS. They would rather pretend it is somebody else's problem. No wonder they don't want leather dykes at the Michigan Womyn's Music Festival. But, like New York City, vanilla dykes are quickly running out of places to put the trash.

Cynthia is in the hospital. I know she is never going to leave. This is the second time she has had pneumonia. She has tubes in her arm. She has tubes in her nose, and I don't want to think about where they go after that. I have talked to the people who hold her medical power of attorney. I have insisted that they stop giving her nutrition and antibiotics. I have insisted that they increase her pain medication. Her boyfriend has accused me of "starving her to death." I keep reminding everyone that it's AIDS that is killing her.

The nurse comes in to brush her teeth. She puts mouthwash on a little pink sponge that's stuck on a stick. Then she runs the sponge between Cynthia's gum and her lip. Cynthia doesn't like it. It hurts her. She tries to turn her head, but she is too doped up to be able to prevent it. Then a technician comes in to take her blood. They want to monitor the levels of the drugs in her bloodstream. She isn't even conscious, but she tries to pull her hand away. I will always be ashamed because I let them brush her teeth and stick her finger to take her blood. What possible difference can it make now? Why can't I be more of a bitch and spare her these petty annoyances?

Her skin is so dry. I take lotion out of the drawer by her bed. I put it on her shoulders, but there's still some left over, so my hands spread it lower down. I have a flash of lesbian paranoia. There is only a curtain between me and the nurse's station. What if the nurses see me fondling this woman's breasts? Then I stifle my fear. If Cynthia could drag my naked ass to parties where dozens of gay men were hanging in slings waiting to get fisted, I can damned well do this for her.

I put lotion on her breasts, her stomach, her thighs. I try not to disturb the catheter. I even put lotion on her feet. It seems to calm her down.

A few weeks ago, she was flirting with me. She wanted to get together and play. I said no, having had too much experience with the way a date with Cynthia turned into a relationship overnight. She was a sarcastic and critical bottom, and I had gotten enough bad reviews from her when I was her lover. She was living with a man who paid her rent and kept her fed and kept her company at night. They weren't having sex. She was contemptuous of him and terrified that he would leave her. I wanted to stay out of the whole fucking mess.

Besides, there wasn't much she could do. She didn't want to get beaten anymore. She had almost no energy. It was hard for her to get fisted. I have always reserved tender sex, the fantasy games about dominance and submission, for my lovers. The games I play with tricks are rougher, physically heavier, easier on the heart and head.

Do I have to tell you that I wish now I had been able to imagine an evening for her, some way to enchant and dazzle her? I doubt I would have succeeded. Real sex always disappointed Cynthia. But it would make me feel better now to know I tried.

In September of 1991, a study of 379 heterosexual couples in San Francisco in which one partner was HIV-positive and the other was not, found that the virus moves from men to women during sex far more easily than it moves from women to men. Unprotected heterosexual intercourse is at least seventeen times more dangerous for women than for men. Nancy Padian, lead author of the study and an assistant professor of epidemiology at the University of California at San Francisco, told the press that she was afraid some heterosexual men would interpret the results of her study to mean they could stop using condoms.

A year later, police are still busting sex workers and giving them mandatory HIV-antibody tests. Newspapers are still whipping the public up about Typhoid Mary hookers who are so irresponsible or drug addicted that they infect their customers. Nobody busts the clients—who are, after all, the ones who have to wear the condoms if prostitutes are not going to get infected. And nobody studies johns to find out why they think it's okay to give their wives and children AIDS.

I guess the results of this study should make me feel better. It would certainly seem to indicate that it's less dangerous to have sex with an HIV-positive woman than with an HIV-positive man. But a low risk is not the same thing as no risk. If women can pass HIV on to their male partners during sex, I believe they can pass it on to me.

An ex-lover in Alaska writes to me, "Everyone here tells me that you died of AIDS two years ago." Then she goes on with her news: where she's working, who she's sleeping with. I can't see the letter; I can only see red.

Last week I went to San Francisco for the International Ms. Leather contest. I had lost some weight. People noticed. I expected compliments. Instead, I got anxious phone calls.

"Are you sick?" Are they really disappointed when I say no, or am I just indulging in paranoia?

When I did research for my lesbian sex manual, *Sapphistry*, in the mid-seventies, none of the doctors I talked to, including lesbian physicians, thought gay women had to worry about VD. I went out on a limb and wrote the chapter on sexually transmitted diseases anyway. The publisher didn't want to include it. Today it's pretty common knowledge that women can give each other just about any STD. But there are still "experts" who claim that AIDS is not on that list. Why? Dr. Charles Schable of the Centers for Disease Control told a reporter at *Visibilities* that "Lesbians don't have much sex." Well! I'm sure we don't have much sex with him.

The fact is that the CDC don't know whether lesbians are at risk for AIDS or not because they don't bother to ask. They don't keep track of us. Despite the absence of any official statistics on lesbians, we've still been able to determine that at least 100 women with AIDS in the CDC's files have reported having sex with other women. Nearly 700 out of 5,000 women's sexual preferences couldn't be categorized because there wasn't enough information on the report forms. The CDC are unable to determine how 23 percent of the women with AIDS became infected. Wouldn't we be a lot more upset if one-fourth of the men who had AIDS became ill for an unknown reason?

Every lesbian health worker I've ever talked to knows or has treated dykes who have AIDS. Many of them die in the closet. Two women I once knew in New York suddenly disappeared. They stopped coming to public functions and quit seeing their friends. Years later, I heard a rumor that one of them had died of AIDS. They were afraid of anybody finding out because the sick woman thought she would lose all her medical benefits from work. The surviving partner is socially active once more, but she refuses to discuss her partner's death. I wonder if she's having safe sex with her new girlfriend.

By my bed, I keep bottles of water-based lubricant, a box of rubber gloves, and Trojans, the brand preferred by lesbians because everybody is allergic to nonoxynol-9, and who wants to put a dildo down your throat that has a lubricated condom on it? The rule is that I will always use latex barriers with tricks. I will have unsafe sex with my lovers, and then only if we both test HIV-negative.

In fact, I hardly ever bring people home anymore. I tell myself it's because I can't deal with the emotional complications. It's easier to keep casual sex partners separate from my lovers if I only have casual sex in public. When I do scenes with people at parties, I usually don't fuck them. I tell myself it's because I don't want them to expect the scene to turn into a relationship. So I wind up using maybe six gloves a year. And suddenly I have a lot more women in my life whom I consider my lovers.

One of my girlfriends calls me to bitch about her slave, Ricki. She just found out that Ricki has been letting her drug dealer—a man who has AIDS—screw her. They are not using condoms. "What do you care?" I say. "You've been using gloves with her, haven't you?" There's no answer. "Haven't you?" I insist.

No, they have not. My lover and I start having that old argument whether or not you can get AIDS from putting your hand in somebody's cunt or in somebody's ass. I accuse her of not caring about me, of being indiscriminate, careless, stupid. I scream at her that she has to go get tested right away, and I hang up on her.

I should be ashamed of myself. The whole thing is stupid. An HIV-antibody test won't fix this. She hasn't done anything with Ricki that I didn't do with my other girlfriends. Do I really think romance will protect me? I'm glad I moved to Los Angeles, where there's nobody I want to have sex with anyway. I haven't written any porn for a year, and I don't care. It's not real fiction anyway. It doesn't matter. Nobody will miss it. Just like I don't miss sex.

A year after Cynthia's death, the mixed-gender S/M organization that she founded, the Society of Janus, asked its membership to vote on whether they should require safe sex at their parties. After bitter debate, the majority voted not to "force" members to have safer sex at Janus events because AIDS isn't an issue for heterosexuals.

A gay male friend who sees the latex stash by my bed tells me sadly, "Gee, I was really hoping that you girls were still carrying on without having to worry about bagging it. I guess I thought if the party was over for us, somebody was still having a good time." I try to tell him I'm still having a good time, but he doesn't want to hear it. The details about what I do with my pussy or anybody else's pussy make him queasy.

When I start telling friends that my new lover has a chronic, debilitating disease of unknown origin, which her doctor will eventually label chronic fatigue immune dysfunction syndrome, many of them advise me to leave her. "Think what a negative impact it will have on the rest of your life," they say. The same friends would be absolutely scathing if two men broke up because one of them could not deal with his boyfriend's AIDS diagnosis.

There are days when my lover is in so much pain and so disoriented that she can't get out of bed and go to the bathroom by herself. We have a running joke about waiting for our Shanti volunteer and our free bag of groceries. But soon we realize that most of our gay male friends have dropped us. I think it's because we are no longer on the list of potential caretakers. The joke isn't funny anymore.

I have become progressively more angry about gay men's ignorance about women's sexuality, bodies, and health issues. I have started talking about the fact that breast cancer is an epidemic. People think I am a crazy separatist. And of course that's the very worst thing you can be—a woman who puts other women first. But I am tired of taking care of men who have no idea what I do to get off, what my other passions might be, why reproductive rights are important, or what I do when I am not picking up their laundry, giving them medicine, or cleaning up their puke.

I have stopped going to AIDS benefits unless the money is earmarked to provide services to women. I even tell one of my gay male friends that if he gets AIDS now, he has no excuse, and I am not going to take care of him. I can't tell if I'm just depressed and burned out, or if I really mean it. In January of 1989, the *New England Journal of Medicine* published a letter from two doctors in Massachusetts about a sixty-year-old man, rendered impotent by diabetes, who seroconverted after having oral sex with an HIV-infected prostitute. He said he'd never had a homosexual encounter, done IV drugs, or even had a blood transfusion. He'd never gone down on her when she was bleeding. I wonder what

Sarah Schulman has to say about his case—that needles and men are lurking in the background?

When I use gloves, when I keep my mouth off somebody's cunt, I feel virtuous the next day. I'm relieved. I can't quite believe I managed to behave myself. But it reminds me too much of the way I used to feel when I believed masturbation was a sin, and I managed to quit (in the middle of raging adolescent hormone storms) for a week or even ten whole days.

I can tell myself it's not the same thing. Safer sex is not a form of prudery. It's not based on hatred of the body, on aversion to bodily fluids, on a fear of sex. I tell myself and I tell myself, but my tongue does not believe what my brain believes. My hand does not believe what my brain believes. I need what lies beyond the barrier.

It took me so many years to understand that I wanted to put my tongue in between another woman's legs. Years more to learn how to do it well enough to make her want to keep me there. When I put my face between my lover's broad thighs, I am hungry for the smell and taste of lesbian desire, and I am making her a promise that what we do with each other is real, it matters, our bodies are valuable and beautiful. I am the kind of girl who prefers to swallow it. It is affirmation and salvation. Sex without that salty taste makes me lonely.

It took me years to believe that my hand working in a woman's cunt could make her come, really satisfy her; years more to be able to strap on a dildo and fuck the way men fuck with a dyke's knowledge of where the hot spots inside a woman's body lie, how the passage inside her ass curves, and how to search out her cries, her wild movements, her desperation, and her fulfillment. I want that slickness between my thumb and forefinger, I want the palpable evidence of my prowess to make my hand wet to the wrist.

In the Spring 1991 issue of *Lesbian Contradiction,* Beth Elliott published an article entitled "Does Lesbian Sex Transmit AIDS? G.E.T. R.E.A.L.!" The acronym stands for "Getting Empowered to Re-Educate the Anti-Lesbian." According to Elliott, being anti-lesbian means saying that lesbian sex transmits the AIDS virus. Elliott believes this is "a fable invested with an aura of fact, like the story of the poodle in the microwave." If gay men "have reopened sex clubs, complete with glory holes, on the theory that fellatio is safe," she wants to know why AIDS activists are telling women to use dental dams during cunnilingus. She believes that "pressuring lesbians to identify with AIDS" is an attempt "to replace lesbian feminism with a forcibly integrated community in which lesbians play the traditional female role." She adds:

> Lesbians are cooperating, but getting no more respect than in the past. Whether from guilt or our upbringing as caregivers we have been uncharacteristically silent while losing our lesbian identity. To the general public, we are just like gay men in life-style, AIDS risk, and sexuality. We are no longer lesbians: we are now Mrs. Homosexual. And our rights are at risk because the best weapon against AIDS backlash lesbians and gay men have—the reality of lesbian lives—is something gay men do not want to face.

When Risa Denenberg wrote an article in the Summer 1991 issue of *Out/Look,* "We Shoot Drugs, and We are Your Sisters," Elliott responded in a letter to the editor: "Giving IV drug users the message that their behavior and culture are welcome in a community aiming to support, empower and validate women...is a very bad idea.... Denenberg doesn't care one bit about lesbians and the women's community."

I overhear a conversation in the hallway at work: "Daniel's HIV-positive," somebody says smugly. Just passing by.

"Well," is the tart reply, "I guess we all know what *she's* been up to now!"

There is no compassion in these voices. I happen to know that one of the men talking already has KS.

Suppose it's true that sexual transmission of HIV from one woman to another is practically nonexistent. Suppose it's true that every lesbian who is HIV-positive got the virus because she had unprotected sex with men or shared needles. What should these women do now—stop having sex? Who thinks it would be safe to put her hand inside one of these women without a glove? Would you put your tongue on her? Would you do it if she was having her period?

Would it help her, do you think, to be told that she is part of a community that has historically behaved in a very faddish manner? Do you think she needs to know that a dental dam really fits into a lot of people's shame about their sexuality? Would her girlfriend be comforted by the information that dental dams have never been tested for efficacy? Do you think at that point that either of them really gives a damn how this disease entered their lives?

Queer Nation girls would hit the streets if the government started rounding up HIV-infected men and shipping them to quarantine camps. But how many of us are doing anything about the invisible quarantine that exists around the bodies of bisexual and lesbian women who have AIDS?

Maybe the handful of dykes who have AIDS are like the handful of men who had PCP in the seventies. Maybe they represent the tip of the iceberg, and ten years from now we will be sorry we didn't anticipate a deluge of lesbian AIDS cases. Maybe not. Maybe there will always be only a few women who have AIDS who want to have sex with and love other women.

There isn't enough money to go around to fight this disease. So is it okay if a dozen women a year die in isolation, and possibly infect others because they don't know any better? How about two dozen? Two hundred? A few thousand? What's an acceptable cutoff point before we divert resources to prevent this tragedy? What's the bottom line? Does it make a difference if these women don't speak English as their first language? —If they are not white? What if they don't call themselves lesbians? Do they have to be in recovery? What if they have children? Maybe they want to have more children. Maybe they used to be hustlers. Maybe they still turn tricks.

It's confusing. It would be so much simpler to think about these issues if women would just be consistent, have simple identities, and stop behaving in complex ways that are affected by their culture and their need to survive. What we need is a little more monogamy and purity and all the other virtues of the white middle class. Including the money. Most of all, we could use the money.

I have someone stretched underneath me. Her hands are tied. I have cut her back, and I suppose I could pretend that I don't intend to put my mouth on the wound I've just made. But this is not an ornamental cut—an orchid, a whip, a snake. It is utilitarian: two short lines that cross each other at right angles. It delays the clotting of blood, which wells up thick as tar, a bead of perfect scarlet. Any second now, it will break and run. It will be wasted.

I have my cock up her ass. The smell, the sounds of ass-fucking are all around me. My hands are wet with sweat and lube. I'm going to come soon, and I put my face down to her back and bite the skin around the cut so the blood spurts into my mouth.

The sight of blood makes most people sick. It means there's an injury, pain, maybe even the possibility of death. But I can smell a woman who is bleeding across a crowded room. I bleed myself every month. I'm not afraid of it. The sight of someone else's blood, my own blood, makes me shake with excitement. It is life. Shedding it and sharing it is the ultimate violation and intimacy for me.

I try to fend off the moment when I have to drink it. I will not cut anybody. Or I will just cut myself. I appreciate my own pain, enjoy the adrenaline it takes to slice my own skin, but my own blood has no taste. So I have to take this need to someone else. But I will just smear it on my skin, my face, where I can smell it, but it isn't in my mouth. If I have to drink it, I'll take it out with a syringe and squirt it into brandy to kill the virus.

But this is tonight; this is urgent. It's been too long. This is something I have to have. I drink with the intensity of a newborn child.

If I get sick tomorrow, will you feel any compassion for me?

A friend of mine says, "Even if I can't catch AIDS from my tricks, I don't want to catch any of the little things either.

There's no cure for herpes, and it's unbelievably painful. Later for that. Check the pockets of my jacket. I always carry lube and rubber."

When I confess that my track record with safer sex is less than perfect, I'm not trying to tell everyone to throw away their condoms. I haven't thrown away my gloves. Someday I'll even try those goddamned dental dams again. Maybe it would make a difference if I used them with somebody I wasn't about to break up with. Maybe Saran Wrap doesn't pull your short hairs out. At least it's transparent.

Most of us are doing the best we can, trying to scrape through this epidemic with as much of our libidos and our sanity as we can rescue. Some of us are celibate. I think of those folks as being shell-shocked by the sex wars. Some of us deliberately do stupid things—like the man I know who won't use condoms because he always pulls out before he comes, and he firmly believes there is no HIV in precome. Or the johns who won't use rubbers with prostitutes. Or the dykes who think they can keep themselves safe by avoiding women in high-risk categories. Some of us know what we should do, we do it most of the time, and sometimes we slip.

We slip because the condition of being aroused creates moisture. Hazardous footing. Melts boundaries. Makes the edges fuzzy. Creates immediate needs that overwhelm our ability to plan for the future. I know I should scold you, punish myself, there probably ought to be a law.

Think about that. No. No. There should not be a law. The desire itself is always honorable. Always. Even if it carries unwelcome microbes along with it, like a Helms amendment riding on a budget bill. Never be sorry that you know what sex tastes like. Never be sorry that you have touched another human being intimately, drawn a part of them into your body. It is worth the price.

I think we must paraphrase that saying about a hard cock having no conscience. When the sexual flesh is hard, engorged, it has no conscience. Gender is not the determining factor. Most of us know only one or two ways to get off. Most of us have a hard time finding somebody we desire who is also able and willing to get us off. There are so many barriers between us—money, time, fear, age, race, violence, shame, inhibition, ignorance. Nobody wants another barrier. It's no wonder that a piece of latex doesn't look like protection. It doesn't look like freedom from anxiety. It looks like another obstacle, another wall we have to break through if we are ever going to inhabit our bodies like free ecstatic animals.

Sex has always been a high-risk activity. I continue to struggle to make it as safe as I possibly can. But I can't lie to myself and pretend that I haven't given something up. And sometimes I just can't make myself believe that the bargain is worth it. And then I slip. When I slip, I do things that endanger my life. But I also find the hope I need to go on compromising, struggling, doing without, and getting by.

## About the Contributors

**Dorothy Allison** ("Believing in Literature") is a lifelong feminist and queer activist. She is the author of the novel *Bastard Out of Carolina,* a National Book Award finalist. She is currently working on a new novel. She's also published a recent book of essays called *Skin,* as well as *Trash*—a double Lambda award winner in fiction, and *The Women Who Hate Me, Poetry: 1980-1990.*

**Pat Califia** ("Slipping") is a major figure in the international leather community. She has published more than a dozen books, in the categories of fiction and nonfiction. Among her titles are included the infamous *Macho Sluts, Doc and Fluff, Sensuous Magic, Public Sex, Doing It for Daddy,* and *Melting Point,* from which the essay "Slipping" has been excerpted.

**Terry Castle** ("First Ed") is a professor of English Literature at Stanford University. She is the author of *Clarissa's Ciphers, The Female Thermometer,* and a book on eighteenth-century English culture and fiction called *Masquerade and Civilization.* The essay "First Ed" comes from her recent book on literary images of lesbians, *The Apparitional Lesbian.*

**Jewelle Gomez** ("Because Silence is Costly") is the author of the award-winning novel, *The Gilda Stories,* about a Black lesbian vampire, and a collection of essays called *Forty-Three Septembers.* Among the anthologies that include her work are *Home Girls, Disorderly Conduct, Reading Black Reading Feminist, The Persistent Desire,* and *Wild Women*

*Don't Wear No Blue.* Her critical writing has appeared in *The New York Times, The Black Scholar, Essence, The Advocate,* and *The Village Voice.* Originally from Boston, she lived in New York City for twenty-two years before coming to San Francisco, where she now resides.

**Judy Grahn** ("How Menstruation Fashioned the Body") is a highly acclaimed poet, playwright, and independent scholar. She has written many mind-altering books, among which are *Blood, Bread, and Roses; Another Mother Tongue; The Queen of Wards, The Queen of Swords; The Work of a Common Woman,* and a novel—*Mundane's World.*

**Judith Halberstam** ("F2M: The Making of Female Masculinity") is an assistant professor of literature at U.C. San Diego where she teaches classes in queer theory, feminist studies, film, and literature. She has a book on Gothic horror forthcoming from Duke University Press and she is presently working on a book about "female masculinity." Articles by her have appeared in *Girlfriends, On Our Backs, Feminist Studies, Camera Obscura,* and *GLQ.*

**Eileen Myles** ("Campaign Diaries") is a writer and performer. Her first collection of fiction, *Chelsea Girls,* came out recently. *Maxfield Parrish, early and new poems* will be published in 1995. Myles has toured Germany with her work and has performed in the United States in many venues ranging from St. Mark's Church, to ICA, The Walker Arts Center, Cal Arts, Naropa Institute, Yale, Brown, and Rutgers. The *New York Times* called her "a highlight" at Lesbopalooza, the world's first lesbian rock festival. She writes a monthly column for *Paper* magazine.

**Jenni Olson** ("Butch Icons of the Silver Screen") is director of the Frameline Archive and Resource Center. As a film collector and archivist, her historical projects, HOMO PROMO (a collection of coming-attraction trailers from lesbian and gay-themed films) and CAMP FOR BOYS AND GIRLS (clips from campy TV shows and movies) have played at lesbian and gay film festivals all over the world. She is the editor of *The Frameline Guide to Films and Videos* featured in the San Francisco International Lesbian and Gay Film Festival, to be published in 1995.

**Robin Podolsky** ("What Can We Make With Fire: What Stories, What Lives") is a writer of fiction, essays, and poetry. Her work has been anthologized in *In a Different Light: An Anthology of Lesbian Writers, Blood Whispers: L.A. Writers on AIDS, Indivisible,* and *Discontents.* She's written for the *L.A. Weekly,* and *The Advocate.* In 1991 she received a special citation from the PEN Center in New York for her book in progress, *Roughing It Out.* In 1991 she received a Media Image Award from GLAAD, and in 1993, a Journalism Award from the NLGJA.

**Camille Roy** ("South Side") is a writer of experimental plays, poetry, and fiction. Her play *Bye Bye Brunhilde* was produced by New Langton Arts and subsequently at Theatre Rhino in San Francisco and at the WOW Café in New York. A book of plays, *Cold Heaven,* was recently published. Her work has appeared in anthologies including *Sisters, Sexperts, Queers.* A new book of selected work, *The Rosy Medallions,* has just been published by Kelsey St. Press.

**Canyon Sam** ("1975: All that Shattered")is a writer, performance artist, teacher, and activist. Her work has been published in numerous journals and anthologies, including *The Very Inside, Out Rage, Lesbian Love Stories, Finding Courage,* and *New Lesbian Writing. Taxi Karma* and *The Dissident,* two pieces from her one-woman show about her journeys in China and Tibet, have toured the country to national acclaim. Her book, *One Hundred Voices of Tara,* about Tibetan women, will be published in 1995–96. Canyon Sam was founder of the first organized group of Asian-American lesbians in the nation, in 1977.

**Randy Turoff** ("Chic by Nature") is currently working on a book of personal essays called *Chic by Nature.* She is also completing a novel. From 1985 to 1994, she was a cultural arts critic for *The San Francisco Bay Times* newspaper. Her articles have also appeared in *Lambda Book Report, The Lesbian Review of Books,* and in literary, film, and travel magazines. In 1990 she received the Wallace Hamilton Award for cultural reporting from the Gay and Lesbian Press Association. As a critic she has served on numerous judging committees for film festivals and literary awards. In the early 1980s, in Provincetown, she was a founding editor of one of the first slick lesbian arts magazines—*Womantide.* Additionally, she has worked extensively in theater as a director and poet/performance artist.

**Andrea Weiss** ("The Vampire Lovers") is a writer and an independent filmmaker with a Ph.D. in American cultural history. She is the author of *Vampires and Violets: Lesbians in Film* (Penguin 1993) and *Paris Was a Woman* (Harper San Franciso, 1995) which is a companion book to the forthcoming documentary film of the same name. Her feature film directorial debut, *A Bit of Scarlet,* will be released in the summer of 1996. Andrea Weiss won an Emmy for her research on the documentary *Before Stonewall.* Her films have won awards at festivals worldwide. She lives in New York City and in London.